BEYOND TRAUMA

A Healing Journey for Women

FACILITATOR'S GUIDE

Stephanie S. Covington

Marcia K. Morgan, Curriculum Designer

HAZELDEN®

Hazelden
Center City, Minnesota 55012-0176

1-800-328-9000
1-651-213-4590 (Fax)
www.hazelden.org

ISBN: 1-59285-068-5

Cover design by David Spohn
Interior design and typesetting by Kinne Design

CONTENTS

ACKNOWLEDGMENTS

Any project I've ever done has had important people behind the scenes, and this curriculum is no exception. I'm very fortunate to be surrounded by caring and competent people who have supported this project from beginning to end.

Sid Farrar, Corrine Casanova, Alex Scott, and Nancy Alliegro are part of the enthusiastic Hazelden team who encouraged this work. Marcia Morgan brought her expertise in curriculum writing to a large volume of materials and ideas. Kary Young spent long hours on the computer and read innumerable drafts for needed changes in tone, content, and process. Carol Ackley donated her time and expertise to the pilot of the curriculum and to the development of the videos. Stephanie Brown, Charles Figley, Martin Horn, and Lisa Najavits were willing to incorporate the manuscript into their busy schedules and generously contribute endorsements. Last but not least, I am indebted to Penny Philpot for sharing her clinical knowledge, technical determination, and sense of humor; and for being an inspiration for this curriculum.

To all of you, I say "Thank You" for your expertise, your support, and your dedication to helping women move *Beyond Trauma*.

INTRODUCTION

As we look around, it seems our world is in a state of crisis. Everywhere we look, we see pain and devastation. Suffering and alienation are reflected in the wars in the Middle East, Latin America, and Africa. Widespread violence can be seen in the growing number of child abuse cases in the United States, the raping of women on every continent, and the international sex trade. Painful destruction is mirrored by the holes in the ozone layer, the clear-cutting of timber in the rain forests, the annihilation of plant and animal species, and our polluted air and water. Violence happens in multiple ways and on many levels.

Where do we look for answers? What is the key to our survival and healing? Just as the Chinese symbol for *crisis* is made up of two characters, one representing danger and the other opportunity, each time there is a crisis there is also a chance for change and renewal. Today many women and men from all walks of life are finding a key to their survival and growth by freeing themselves from the suffering created by trauma.

Though we see violence everywhere we look, we need to make a distinction between the suffering that we create and the suffering that we encounter as a natural part of our lives. Certainly, we cannot avoid the suffering that comes from natural disasters, such as earthquakes, floods, and tornadoes. We also often experience pain during the normal course of life, as we are born, grow up, get an education, move into the workplace and relationships, age, and experience death. Though these passages can be difficult, they are also the foundation stones of our identities. They challenge us, helping us to define who we are and what we want from our lives. We can see these kinds of experiences as a part of life's journey and use them to help us grow and create meaning in our lives.

At the other end of the spectrum is the suffering that we, as human beings, have created—the abuse and destruction generated by violence. Wherever we look, around the world and at every level of our own society, we can see the pain and destruction that results from created violence. Every day in America, women are sexually harassed in the workplace, raped, and beaten by their husbands, boyfriends, and strangers. Increasing numbers of our children are neglected, abused, and killed by their parents and caretakers. No institution, person, or country is free from the effects of created suffering.

However, there is hope. Already in our world today, individuals and groups are coming together to create new ways of ending suffering. One of the first steps on this new path is freeing ourselves from denial and acknowledging the impact of violence in our society. One can only heal from a problem that has been named.

This curriculum, *Beyond Trauma: A Healing Journey for Women,* has been designed to be part of the solution by helping women to recover from the impact of trauma in their lives. The curriculum focuses on the kinds of created suffering that women are most at risk of experiencing: childhood abuse, rape, battering, and other forms of interpersonal violence. However, the coping skills that we will cover in Module C can also be useful for other types of traumatic events.

Beyond Trauma presents an integrated approach to women's treatment, based on theory, research, and clinical experience. It can be used in any setting (outpatient, residential, therapeutic community, criminal justice, or private practice). In developing effective treatment for women, we must include the experience and impact of living as a woman in a male-based society—in other words, gender—as part of the clinical perspective. The term *gender-responsive* describes this type of treatment approach and is defined as follows: creating an environment through site selection, program development, content, and material that reflects an understanding of the realities of women's lives and is responsive to the issues of the clients (Covington 2002). *Beyond Trauma* is a gender-responsive curriculum.

This curriculum promotes a strength-based approach that seeks to empower women and increase their sense of self. In using this kind of model, you, the facilitator, will help the women in the group to see the strengths they have and to increase the skills they need for healing. The curriculum also focuses on emotional development. Dealing with the expression and containment of feelings is a critical part of trauma work. You will be using psychoeducational and cognitive-behavioral techniques (CBT), expressive arts, and relational therapy.

The *Beyond Trauma* program materials consist of a facilitator's guide, a participant's workbook, two facilitator training videos, and one client video.

This facilitator's guide has five parts, but it's essentially divided into two halves. The first half gives you some background information about trauma. Having a basic understanding of the depth and complexity of the issues will help you facilitate the group process. The second half of the guide includes Session Outlines, which are like lesson plans. There is a total of eleven sessions in the three modules: (A) Violence, Abuse, and Trauma; (B) The Impact of Trauma on Women's Lives; and (C) Healing from Trauma.

The women in the group will go through a process of

1. understanding what has happened to them. They will learn more about what abuse is and how widespread abuse is in women's lives.

2. exploring how abuse has impacted them.

3. learning coping mechanisms, doing exercises to help them feel grounded, and focusing on safety.

Some of you may also be facilitating the *Helping Women Recover: A Program for Treating Addiction* curriculum (the community or criminal justice version). The *Beyond Trauma* curriculum can be used alone or in addition to *Helping Women Recover (HWR)*. These programs are complementary to each other, and *Beyond Trauma* expands and deepens the trauma work in *HWR*.

Thank you for making the decision to help facilitate the process of the healing journey for women. Although you may find this work particularly challenging, it will also reward you. Many of you are recovering from trauma yourself and know that there is no more powerful transformation than that of a woman reclaiming her life.

Stephanie S. Covington

Stephanie S. Covington
November 2003
La Jolla, California

PART ONE

BACKGROUND INFORMATION

✺ What Is Trauma? ✺

Violence-related trauma occurs on multiple levels, from the general and chronic oppression of an entire group of people—through discrimination based on gender, race, poverty, sexual orientation, gender identity, disability, or age—to the repeated sexual abuse of a child that continues over several years. Violence and trauma take many forms, including emotional, physical, and sexual abuse, as well as assault, war, natural disasters, and political terrorism.

The Diagnostic and Statistical Manual of Mental Disorders, or *DSM-IV-TR (Text Revision),* defines *trauma* as "involving direct personal experience of an event that involves actual or threatened death or serious injury, or other threat to one's physical integrity; or witnessing an event that involves death, injury, or a threat to the physical integrity of another person; or learning about unexpected or violent death, serious harm, or threat of death or injury experienced by a family member or other close associate. The person's response to the event must involve intense fear, helplessness, or horror (or in children, the response must involve disorganized or agitated behavior)" (American Psychiatric Association 2000, 463).

In the introduction, two categories of suffering are discussed: natural suffering and created suffering. Natural suffering comes from the normal course of life and from natural disasters. Created suffering is created by human beings. Sometimes researchers distinguish between three types of traumatic events: disaster, assaults, and combat (Winfield et al. 1990; Cottler et al. 1992). Others discuss accidental and intentional disasters and the resulting trauma (Godleski 1997). Still others define trauma not as an event but as a reaction to an event that overwhelms people physically and psychologically (Levine 1997). So the word *trauma* is used both to describe an event and to describe a reaction or response to an event.

There are also differences between women and men in terms of trauma. Compared to men, women are more likely to be exposed to physical abuse, rape, sexual molestation, childhood parental neglect, and childhood physical abuse (Cottler, Nishith, and Compton 2001; Kessler et al. 1999; Triffleman 1998). In fact, violence against women is so pervasive that the United Nations has addressed and defined violence against women as "any act of gender-based violence that results in, or is likely to result in, physical, sexual, or psychological harm or suffering to women, including threats of such acts, coercion, or arbitrary deprivations of liberty, whether occurring in public or private life" (United Nations General Assembly 1993).

⧼ Women and Trauma ⧽

The World Women Live In

The following statistics illustrate how pervasive interpersonal violence is in the lives of women and girls.

- The strongest risk factor for being a victim of partner violence is being female (American Psychological Association 1996).

- Approximately 1.5 million women are raped or physically assaulted by an intimate partner each year in the United States. Because many victims are victimized more than once, approximately 4.8 million intimate partner rapes and physical assaults against women are committed annually (Bureau of Justice Statistics [BJS] 2000a).

- Violence against the woman occurs in approximately 20 percent of dating couples (American Psychological Association 1996).

- Women aged sixteen to twenty-four experience the highest per capita rates of intimate violence (19.6 victimizations per 1,000 women) (BJS 2003).

- Violence within the family is traumatizing to most women. Even a single act of violence by a family member may cause long-lasting trauma as well as immediate harm to a female victim observer (American Psychological Association 1996).

- "While both male and female children are at risk for abuse, females continue to be at risk for interpersonal violence in their adolescence and adult lives." The risk for males to be abused in their teenage and adult relationships is far less than for females (Covington and Surrey 1997, 341).

- In 1998, more than 1,800 murders in the United States were attributed to intimate partners. Three-quarters of the victims were women, accounting for 33 percent of all murders of women and 4 percent of all murders of men (BJS 2000a).

- More female than male adolescents have been sexually assaulted. One study reported assaults on 13 percent of females compared to 3.4 percent of males (Kilpatrick and Saunders 1997); another reported assaults on 38 percent of females and 7 percent of males (Commonwealth Fund 1997).

- An estimated 67 of every 100,000 females in the United States were reported rape victims in 1998. Despite a decline in the nation's crime rate over the past decade, reported rates of rape and sexual assault did not decline (FBI 1999).

- Only 22 percent of rapes are committed by someone the victim does not know (Kilpatrick et al. 1998).

- While relationship violence happens to women of every race and ethnic background, African American women are physically assaulted at a rate that is 35 percent higher than Caucasian women and about two and a half times the rate of women of other races (National Coalition Against Domestic Violence 2000).

- One-third of women in state prisons and one-fourth of women in jails said they had been raped (BJS 1999).

- Women in prison reported childhood abuse at a rate almost twice that of men; abuse of women as adults was eight times higher than the rate for men (Messina, Burdon, and Prendergast 2001).

- Between 23 and 37 percent of female offenders reported that they had been physical or sexually abused before the age of eighteen (BJS 1999).

As mentioned before, trauma occurs on multiple levels. "Trauma is not limited to suffering violence; it includes witnessing violence, as well as stigmatization because of gender, race, poverty, incarceration, or sexual orientation" (Covington 2002, 60). M. Root also expands the conventional notion of trauma to include not only direct trauma but also indirect trauma and insidious trauma. Insidious trauma "includes but is not limited to emotional abuse, racism, anti-Semitism, poverty, heterosexism, dislocation, [and] ageism" (1992, 23). The effects of insidious trauma are cumulative and are often experienced over the course of a lifetime. For example, women of color are subject to varying degrees of insidious trauma throughout their lives. According to Root, the exposure to insidious trauma activates survival behaviors that might be easily mistaken for pathological responses if their source is not understood. Misdiagnosis of pathology can be a consequence of a lack of understanding of the impact of insidious trauma on women who have lived their lives under the impact of racism, heterosexism, and/or class discrimination.

❧ Understanding Trauma ❧

The women in your group may be at various stages in facing and dealing with their abuse. Some will remember their abuse clearly, some will remember certain aspects, and some will not remember anything. Some will talk openly about their abuse right away, and some will not. Because women are at different stages and because all need to feel safe, you will begin by normalizing the existence of interpersonal violence. Therefore, Module A is focused on the prevalence of violence in women's lives. For facilitators who have little or no experience working with trauma, Figure 1 on the next page will help you to understand the process of trauma.

Process of Trauma

Trauma begins with an event or experience that overwhelms a woman's normal coping mechanisms. The first response that a person has when threatened is either fight or flight. Then there are physiological and psychological reactions in response to the event: hyperarousal, altered consciousness, numbing, and so on. These are normal reactions to an abnormal situation. There are changes in the brain, and a woman's nervous system also becomes sensitized and is vulnerable to any future stressors in her life. She may experience triggers in her current life by reminders of the traumatic event that happened in the past. There may be nightmares and flashbacks to the earlier experience. This creates a painful emotional state and subsequent behavior. The behaviors we often see can be placed into three categories: retreat, self-destructive action, and destructive action. Women are more likely to retreat or be self-destructive, while men are more likely to engage in destructive behavior. Women often internalize their feelings and men often externalize theirs.

FIGURE 1

Trauma Process

Traumatic Event

Overwhelms the physical and psychological systems

Response to Trauma

Fight or flight, freeze, altered state of consciousness, body sensations,
numbing, hypervigilance, hyperarousal

Sensitized Nervous System

Changes in the Brain

Current Stress

Reminders of trauma, life events, lifestyle

Painful Emotional State

Retreat	**Self-Destructive Action**	**Destructive Action**
Isolation	Substance abuse	Aggression
Dissociation	Eating disorders	Violence
Depression	Deliberate self-harm	Rages
Anxiety	Suicidal actions	

Disorders Related to Trauma

One of the most important developments in health care over the past several decades is the recognition that a substantial proportion of people have a history of serious traumatic experiences that play a vital, and often unrecognized, role in the evolution of an individual's physical and mental health problems.

Disorders that are related to trauma include post-traumatic stress disorder (PTSD), brief reactive psychosis, dissociative identity disorder, dissociative fugue, dissociative amnesia, conversion disorder, depersonalization disorder, somatization disorder, dream anxiety disorder, and antisocial personality disorder.

There is also a high level of comorbidity in women between post-traumatic stress and other disorders: depression, anxiety, panic disorder, phobic disorder, substance abuse, and physical disorders (Davidson 1993).

The symptoms of post-traumatic stress disorder are a common experience for many victims of abuse. It will be helpful for you to be familiar with the symptoms of PTSD and with the criteria for resolving it. The *Diagnostic and Statistical Manual of Mental Disorders IV (DSM-IV)* of the American Psychiatric Association lists some of the symptoms of PTSD (1994, 427–29) as

- reexperiencing the event through nightmares and flashbacks

- avoidance of stimuli associated with the event (for example, if a woman was raped in a park, she may avoid parks, or if she was assaulted by a blond man, she may avoid men with blond hair)

- estrangement (the inability to be emotionally close to anyone)

- numbing of general responsiveness (feeling nothing most of the time)

- hypervigilance (constantly scanning one's environment for danger, whether physical or emotional)

- exaggerated startle response (a tendency to jump at loud noises or unexpected touch)

However, when you discuss the effects of abuse with women, you will probably want to speak less technically. For example, here are the three basic reactions:

1. reexperiencing (includes disturbed sleep, intrusive memories, distressing dreams, nightmares, flashbacks, reliving the event, a view of the world as unsafe)

2. numbing and avoidance (mistrust of others, isolation and disconnection, emotional numbness, low self-esteem, neglect of health, dissociation, ability to remember events or feelings but not both, memory loss for certain events, loss of faith and hope)

3. hyperarousal (intense emotions, difficulty sleeping, panic and anxiousness, self-harm, risky behaviors, irritability, anger, difficulty concentrating)

There are two types of PTSD: simple and complex. Simple PTSD is from a single incident (such as an earthquake or auto accident), usually as an adult. Complex PTSD is from repeated incidents (such as childhood sexual abuse or domestic violence). Generally, there are more symptoms and a more complicated recovery process with the complex PTSD (Herman 1997; Najavits 2002).

The *DSM-IV-TR* uses DESNOS (disorder of extreme stress, not otherwise specified) for a diagnosis of complex PTSD. Figure 2 on page 12 shows the symptoms of PTSD, with examples of how women may experience the symptoms and some clinical tips for responding.

It is also important to acknowledge the long-term effects of trauma. Traumatic events may affect women for the rest of their lives. However, there are criteria you can use when assessing a woman's recovery. Healing from trauma means the following (Harvey 1996):

- The physical symptoms of PTSD are within manageable limits.

- The person is able to bear feelings associated with traumatic memories.

- The person has authority over her memories (that is, her memories don't limit what she does; she chooses what to do, instead of being immobilized in some areas).

- Memory of trauma is linked with feelings.

- Damaged self-esteem is restored (for example, a rape victim realizes that the rape did not occur because she was a "bad" woman).

- Important relationships have been reestablished.

- The person has reconstructed a system of meaning and belief that encompasses the story of the trauma (for instance, she understands that the rape was not caused by her and that some men use power and control to get what they want).

FIGURE 2

Post-Traumatic Stress Disorder Symptoms

SYMPTOMS	CLIENT EXPERIENCE	CLINICAL TIP
Reexperiencing: *Flashbacks, nightmares*	• Client feels tossed out of the present and thrown back into the nightmare world of the past	• Grounding • Relaxation techniques • Education about trauma for both client and clinician • CBT and self-help
Numbing and Avoidance: *Staying away from persons, places, and things that remind client of trauma*	• Disconnection from others and one's own feelings • "Death in life" experience • Mechanical experience of life; matter-of-fact discussion of painful events • Isolation; profound loneliness • Use of this as an ineffective defense against overwhelming feelings	• Understand this as an ineffective defense against overwhelming feelings • Clinician regulates closeness/distance to create sense of safety • CBT groups
Hyperarousal: *Heightened startle response; heightened aggression*	• All-or-none thinking • Suspicion regarding relationships • Terror of being over-whelmed by feelings or controlled by others	• Knowledge of symptoms • Ability to reassure and contain • Increase coping and self-soothing capacities • CBT

(Cramer 2000.)

Common Responses to Trauma

A traumatic event can impact a person in multiple ways. It can impact both the inner self and the outer self. When it impacts the inner part of the self, it impacts thoughts, feelings, beliefs, and values. For example, some women believe that "you can't trust anyone," and "the world is a very unsafe place."

It can also impact the outer self, which consists of our relationships and behavior. Many women who have experienced trauma struggle with their relationships—with families, friends, and sexual partners. For example, parenting is a relationship that can become even more complicated by the experience of trauma. Some women who have experienced childhood abuse may find their own child "triggers" them back to their abuse. It is particularly risky when a woman's child becomes the age she was when the abuse began.

Figure 3 (on page 14) can help you see how some of the common responses may appear in a client. We see that trauma impacts both the inner and outer self.

Trauma and the Brain

Some of the most exciting recent advances in the trauma field come from studies of the biological aspects of PTSD. It has become clear that exposure to trauma can have lasting effects on the endocrine, autonomic, and central nervous systems. New studies are finding complex changes in both the function and structure of specific areas of the brain. For example, abnormalities have been found in the brain structures that link fear and memory (van der Kolk 1996).

Dissociation has also been a focus of many of the laboratory studies. We now know that people who enter a dissociative state at the time of trauma are at greater risk for PTSD. It also appears that dissociation, a term initially developed through clinical observation, is a neurobiological process. It is important for clinicians to understand that the brain chemistry responses to trauma can predispose a woman to alcohol and drug abuse, eating disorders, self-harming behavior, and other mental health problems. In addition, when trauma occurs in childhood, it can have lasting effects on the way the brain develops (Herman 1997; Teicher 2002).

Duplicating this page is illegal. Do not copy this material without written permission from the publisher.

13

FIGURE 3

Common Responses to Childhood Trauma among Adults

DOMAIN	REEXPERIENCING-RELATED RESPONSES	AVOIDANCE-RELATED RESPONSES
Cognitive *(inner)*	• Intrusive thoughts • Intrusive images	• Amnesia • Depersonalization • Dissociation
Affective *(inner)*	• Anger • Anxiety/nervousness • Depression • Shame • Hopelessness • Loneliness	• Emotional numbing • Isolation of affect
Behavioral *(outer)*	• Increased activity • Aggression • High tolerance for inappropriate behavior	• Avoidance of trauma-related situations (e.g., through sleep, substance abuse)
Physiological *(inner)*	• Arousal-autonomic • Hyperactivity to trauma triggers	• Sensory numbing • Absence of normal reaction to events
Multiple Domains	• Flashbacks • Age regression • Nightmares	• Complex activities in dissociated states

(Adapted from Whitfield 1995.)

Substance Abuse and Trauma

A history of abuse drastically increases the likelihood that a woman will abuse alcohol and other drugs. Researchers have found that a history of family violence may be the single most influential risk factor for abuse of alcohol and drugs by both women and men (American Psychological Association 1996). In one of the earliest comparison studies of women who were alcoholics and women who were not (Covington and Kohen 1984), 74 percent of the alcoholic women had experienced sexual abuse, 52 percent reported physical abuse, and 72 percent reported emotional abuse. In contrast, 50 percent of the women who were not alcoholics reported sexual abuse, 34 percent reported physical abuse, and 44 percent reported emotional abuse.

Other clinical studies of women in substance abuse treatment programs have documented that up to 75 percent of this population have a history of physical and/or sexual abuse (Roberts 1998; Teusch 1997). Females who abuse substances are estimated to have a 30 to 59 percent rate of current post-traumatic stress disorder (Najavits et al. 1998), which is higher compared to men who abuse substances (Brown and Wolfe 1994). In addition, a history of sexual and/or physical abuse puts women at risk for psychiatric hospitalization (Carmen 1995), depression (Herman 1992; Mirowsky and Ross 1995), eating disorders (Herman 1992; Janes 1994), and self-inflicted injury (Dallam 1997; Miller and Guidry 2001).

The connection between interpersonal violence and substance use and abuse is often complex, especially for women. Survivors of abuse can become dependent on alcohol and/or other drugs in part as a way of managing trauma symptoms and reducing tension and stress from living in violent situations. Men who abuse substances are at risk of violence against women and children, and women who use substances are also more vulnerable to violence because of relationships with others who abuse substances, impaired judgment while using alcohol or drugs, and presence in risky and violence-prone situations. Thus begins a cycle of "victimization, chemical use, retardation of emotional development, limited stress resolution, more chemical use, and heightened vulnerability to further victimization" (Steele 2000, 72).

Consequently, any substance abuse treatment program for women must take into account that most women will have suffered abuse (Covington 2002). Counselors and others need to understand that they are probably treating trauma survivors. For example, many addicted women have been considered "treatment failures" because they relapsed. Now they can be better understood as trauma survivors who returned to alcohol or other drugs in order to medicate the pain of trauma. The vast majority of women who are entering recovery for addiction have experienced some form of abuse: emotional, physical, and/or sexual. Our increased understanding of trauma offers new treatment possibilities for substance-abusing trauma survivors (Covington 1999; Miller and Guidry 2001; Najavits 2002).

Integrated Treatment Approach

The connection between addiction and trauma for women is intricate and not easily disentangled. A treatment provider cannot assume that one is a primary problem and the other secondary. Nor is it always beneficial to delay working on trauma symptoms until the client has been abstinent for a minimum time.

One of the counselor's major functions in treating a woman in recovery with a trauma history is to acknowledge to the woman the connection between substance abuse and violence. This explanation helps to validate a woman's experience, confirming that she is not alone and clarifying that her experience is not shameful. Sharing prevalence data, for example, can help reduce her sense of isolation and shame (Finkelstein 1996).

Women who have been exposed to trauma and are addicted to alcohol or other drugs are also at higher risk for mental disorders. In a review of studies that examined the combined effects of PTSD and substance abuse, Najavits, Weiss, and Shaw (1997) found more comorbid mental disorders, medical problems, psychological symptoms, inpatient admissions, interpersonal problems; lower levels of functioning, compliance with aftercare, and motivation for treatment; and other significant life problems (such as homelessness, HIV, domestic violence, and loss of custody of children) among those with both PTSD and substance abuse, compared to those with one of those problems alone.

Co-occurring disorders are complex, and the historic division in the fields of mental health and substance abuse often has resulted in contradictory treatment. Women in early recovery often show symptoms of mood disorders, but these can be temporary conditions associated with withdrawal from drugs. Also, it is difficult to know whether a psychiatric disorder existed before a woman began to abuse alcohol or other drugs, or whether the psychiatric problem emerged after the onset of substance abuse (Institute of Medicine 1990). In addition, there is the connection between trauma and the symptoms of mental illness (Carmen 1995; Davidson 1993).

Gender differences exist in the behavioral manifestations of mental illness; men generally turn anger outward and women turn it inward. Men tend to be more physically and sexually threatening and assaultive, while women tend to be more depressed, self-abusive, and suicidal. Women engage more often in self-harming behaviors, such as cutting, as well as in verbally abusive and disruptive behaviors.

Given the complexity of and interrelationship between substance abuse, trauma, and mental health in women's lives, it is critical that services become integrated. Researchers and clinicians consistently recommend an integrated model as "more likely to succeed, more effective, and more sensitive to clients' needs" (Najavits, Weiss, and Shaw 1997, 279). A more integrated approach also addresses women's multiple roles, complex psychological identities, and the cultural and social realities in which they live and work as individuals, mothers, daughters, and partners (Minkoff 1989).

⌖ Working with Trauma ⌖

Trauma-Informed Services

Trauma has become so prevalent in our society that we now realize that any system that works with people needs to become trauma informed.

Trauma-informed services are those that take into account the knowledge about violence against women and its impact on their lives. By doing so, a facilitator or therapist is much more effective in providing services. Trauma-informed services

- take the trauma into account
- avoid triggering trauma reactions and/or traumatizing the individual
- adjust the behavior of counselors, other staff, and the organization to support the individual's coping capacity
- allow survivors to manage their trauma symptoms successfully so that they are able to access, retain, and benefit from services (Harris and Fallot 2001)

It is important that the agency or system that you are working in becomes trauma informed. This will help you get the support you'll need and want for facilitating *Beyond Trauma: A Healing Journey for Women.*

The Therapeutic Environment

In the therapeutic process, the environment becomes the foundation for a corrective experience and is a cornerstone in the healing process. The importance of environment is stressed in the field of child psychology (Winnecott 1965; Stern 1985), which demonstrates that the optimum context for childhood development consists of a safe, nurturing, consistent environment where the child experiences warmth and a sense of being cared for and understood. These are the same environmental qualities needed in trauma work.

The therapeutic milieu model provides an example of the environmental context needed for trauma survivors. The term *therapeutic milieu* means a carefully arranged environment that is designed to reverse the effects of exposure to situations characterized by interpersonal violence. This therapeutic culture contains the following five elements (Haigh 1999), all of them fundamental in both community and institutional settings:

- *attachment:* a culture of belonging
- *containment:* a culture of safety
- *communication:* a culture of openness
- *involvement:* a culture of participation and citizenship
- *agency:* a culture of empowerment

The environment in many criminal justice settings is particularly challenging for women with trauma histories. One psychiatrist argues, "We have come to believe that retraumatizing people by placing them in environments that reinforce helplessness, scapegoating, isolation, and alienation must be viewed as antitherapeutic, dangerous, immoral, and a violation of basic human rights" (Bloom 2000, 85).

Any therapeutic process will be unsuccessful if the environment mimics the behaviors of the dysfunctional systems the women have already experienced. Rather, the design of program and treatment strategies should be aimed at undoing some of the prior damage. A therapeutic environment's norms are consciously designed to be different: Safety with oneself and with others is paramount, and the entire environment is designed to create living and learning opportunities for everyone involved, staff and clients alike. *Sanctuary* is the word that best describes the ideal environment (Bloom 2000).

Trauma Treatment

Trauma treatment can be divided into present-focused approaches and past-focused approaches. Present-focused approaches are designed to help women function more effectively by developing coping skills, correcting distorted thinking, and instilling hope. Past-focused treatment approaches encourage women to examine in detail their traumatic experiences in order to eliminate their traumatic stress reactions.

The *Beyond Trauma* curriculum is a present-focused treatment that also allows women to look at the past. It uses a variety of therapeutic approaches, including psychoeducational, cognitive-behavioral, expressive, and relational. The psychoeducational approach is one of the first steps in trauma treatment. It is a core component. This helps women begin to link some of their current difficulties to their trauma histories. Also, many women do not know what abuse is or its impact. For example, learning about PTSD often elicits these responses from women: "Oh, someone knows about this? I've been hiding this for years." "I just thought I was crazy." Many women express relief when they find out that their thoughts, feelings, and behaviors are normal responses to abnormal or extreme events.

Stages of Recovery

Over the past hundred years, there have been a number of studies of trauma, with various experts writing about the process of trauma recovery (Herman 1992, 1997). It is now understood that there are commonalities between rape survivors and combat veterans, between battered women and political prisoners, and between survivors of concentration camps and survivors of abuse in the home. Because the traumatic syndromes have basic features in common, the recovery and healing process also follows a common pathway.

Some theorists have based their constructs on a stage model of recovery, describing the stages in different language but referring to the same process. Essentially, in this model, recovery unfolds in a series of stages. The central task in the first stage of Dr. Judith Herman's model is establishing safety; in the second stage, experiencing remembrance and mourning; and in the third stage, reconnecting with ordinary life (Herman 1992, 1997; see Figure 4). There are several treatment models based on this three-stage process (Bloom 2000; Covington 1999; Najavits 2002).

Figure 5, shown on the next page, indicates the type of group structure and therapeutic process that Dr. Herman recommends for each stage of trauma recovery work.

FIGURE 4

Trauma: Stages of Recovery

SYNDROME	STAGE ONE	STAGE TWO	STAGE THREE
Hysteria (Janet 1889)	Stabilization, symptom-oriented treatment	Exploration of traumatic memories	Personality reintegration, rehabilitation
Combat trauma (Scurfield 1985)	Trust, stress management, education	Reexperiencing trauma	Integration of trauma
Complicated post-traumatic disorder (Brown and Fromm 1986)	Stabilization	Integration of memories	Development of self, drive integration
Multiple personality disorder (Putman 1989)	Diagnosis, stabilization, communication, cooperation	Metabolism of trauma	Resolution, integration, development of postresolution coping skills
Traumatic disorders (Herman 1992)	Safety	Remembrance and mourning	Reconnection

(Adapted from *Trauma and Recovery* by Judith Lewis Herman. Copyright 1997 by Perseus Books Group. Reprinted with permission of Perseus Books Group in the format Trade Book via Copyright Clearance Center.)

FIGURE 5

Trauma: Three Group Models

GROUP	RECOVERY: STAGE ONE	RECOVERY: STAGE TWO	RECOVERY: STAGE THREE
Therapeutic task	Safety	Remembrance and mourning	Reconnection
Time and orientation	Present	Past	Present, future
Focus	Self-care	Trauma	Interpersonal relationships
Membership	Homogeneous	Homogeneous	Heterogeneous
Boundaries	Flexible, inclusive	Closed	Stable, slow turnover
Cohesion	Moderate	Very high	High
Conflict tolerance	Low	Low	High
Time limit	Open-ended or repeating	Fixed limit	Open-ended
Structure	Didactic	Goal-directed	Unstructured
Example	Twelve Step programs	Survivor group	Interpersonal psychotherapy group

(Adapted from *Trauma and Recovery* by Judith Lewis Herman. Copyright 1997 by Perseus Books Group. Reprinted with permission of Perseus Books Group in the format Trade Book via Copyright Clearance Center.)

The Upward Spiral: A Transformational Model

The Upward Spiral model provides another way of thinking about trauma and healing. Instead of the more linear stages of recovery model, the spiral shows the circularity and complexity of trauma work. (See Figure 6.) The downward spiral represents the limitations and constrictions trauma can create in a woman's life. The line through the middle represents the traumatic event. It becomes the organizing principle in her life. There is a turning point, a place of change, at the bottom of the downward spiral. Here a woman steps onto a new path—the upward spiral. The upward spiral represents the process of healing, in which a woman's life begins to expand. The trauma is still the line through the middle, but it has less of an influence; it's loosened its grip. There is space now for new activities and new relationships. The trauma becomes a thread in the tapestry of her life; it is no longer the core. The image of the spiral helps us to see that healing is a transformative process.

FIGURE 6

Spiral of Trauma and Healing
(Transformation)

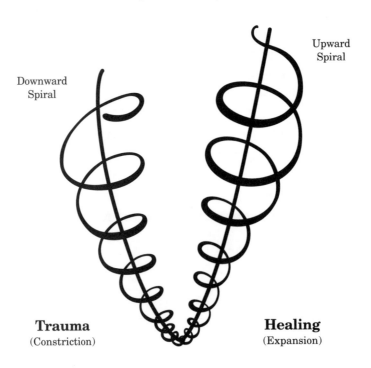

Downward
Spiral

Upward
Spiral

Trauma
(Constriction)

Healing
(Expansion)

(Adapted from *Helping Women Recover.* Copyright 1999 by S. Covington. This material is used by permission of John Wiley & Sons, Inc.)

Creating Safety

Safety is a critical and primary element in trauma work. It is fundamental in all models. Stage One recovery in the Herman model focuses on self-care in the present (see Figure 5). An example of a Stage One group is a Twelve Step group. Stage One groups should be homogeneous (i.e., all women). Stage Two recovery groups focus on the trauma that occurred in the past. The participants tell their stories of trauma and mourn their old selves, which the traumas destroyed. An example of a Stage Two group is a survivors group. Psycho-dynamically focused psychotherapy groups, which traditionally are unstructured and heterogeneous, reflect the third stage of recovery: reconnection. In this stage, the survivors face the task of developing new selves and creating futures for themselves. The group models appropriate to each stage are outlined in Figure 5.

Stage One—safety—is the stage to which facilitators of this program need to be most attuned. It addresses the participants' safety concerns in all the domains identified by Herman. The typical woman entering a substance abuse treatment program is in Stage One; that is, her primary need is safety. *Beyond Trauma* includes sessions that discuss abuse directly, but safety is the priority for the participants throughout the program. In fact, women spend their lives negotiating their safety in various settings.

Facilitators can help the women in the group feel safe by trying to keep the treatment program free of physical, emotional, and sexual harassment and by assessing the risk of domestic violence when the woman returns to her home. Facilitators will also help the women to feel safe internally by teaching them grounding and self-soothing techniques. As stated previously, many trauma survivors use alcohol and/or other drugs to medicate their depression or anxiety because they know no better way to comfort themselves.

Herman emphasizes that a trauma survivor who is working on safety issues needs to be in a homogeneous group. This means that it is important that the group be composed solely of women and that the facilitator be female. Women may not want to talk in depth about physical or sexual abuse in groups that include men until they are ready for a Stage Three trauma recovery group. Coed programs seldom prioritize women's needs or foreground women's talents. Research indicates that single-sex groups are the modality of choice, particularly for women in substance abuse treatment and for trauma survivors

(Aries 1976; McWilliams and Stein 1987; Herman 1992). Women in coed groups often participate less and defocus from self. Although mixed groups (heterogeneous) may have their place later in a woman's recovery, all-female groups help women to develop self-esteem, validate their experiences, and become empowered.

For those working in correctional settings, it is important to acknowledge that abuse can occur in correctional settings as well as in the free world (Covington 1998b). Safety is not guaranteed in the jail, prison, or probation/parole environment, just as it is not guaranteed in the outside world. While a facilitator cannot ensure a woman's safety outside the group, she can maintain an atmosphere of safety within the group. Confidentiality is essential for a sense of psychological safety. What is said in the group remains in the group unless it involves a threat to a woman's safety or that of someone else. In order to help ensure confidentiality in a criminal justice setting, the facilitator may provide time in the group setting for women to do their workbook exercises. Think about how, in your particular environment, you can provide safety by creating options for storing the workbooks. Then women need not worry about having them read by others.

Safety is so crucial for women in early recovery that we will refer to it repeatedly throughout this program. It is important to recognize not only the need for safety but also the lack of it in women's lives. This is a social problem, not just an individual one. While safety is a core element of *Beyond Trauma,* the women will also have an opportunity to begin Stage Two: remembrance and mourning. There are exercises to help them reflect on their trauma history and their experience of loss.

Triggers and Retraumatization

A trigger is a stimulus that sets off a memory of the trauma. That is, a single environmental cue related to the trauma—such as a noise, a sound, a smell, another person's presence—can trigger full fight or flight responses. Profound dysregulation of psychological and physiological systems is a result of trauma and leaves women both overresponding to neutral cues and underresponding to danger cues. Traumatized women are therefore at increased risk of similar and repeated victimization.

Triggering is inevitable; retraumatization is not. Because clients may be naturally triggered in a therapeutic group setting, attention should be paid to increasing the client's attention, care, and coping skills for managing emotional distress (Najavits 2002). Trauma survivors are used to having their boundaries ignored and their opinions or objections dismissed. A crucial element of successful treatment involves attention to these components of women's experience in treatment (Harris and Fallot 2001):

- boundary violations
- lying and breaking integrity
- chaotic treatment environment
- lockstep-rigid agency policies that do not allow a woman to have what she needs
- agency dysfunction
- disruption in routines
- secrets in the group
- not listening to the woman
- not believing her account of the abuse
- labeling intense rage and other feelings as pathological
- minimizing, discrediting, or ignoring the woman's responses
- conducting urinalysis in a nonprivate and disrespectful manner
- stripping a client (such as a woman offender) with male correctional officers present

Dissociation and Grounding

Women who have experienced trauma, particularly in childhood, often learn how to separate themselves from the distress associated with the trauma by using a process called *dissociation*. Dissociation is a mental process, a psychological response that disconnects the mind and the body. When women dissociate, they seem to watch from a distance to maintain a sense of what's happening without having to be part of the experience. For example, while you are facilitating the group, you may have women who are attending the group but periodically "aren't there." They have psychologically left the group. Women often experience dissociation as "losing time." Dissociation is a common response to a trigger (e.g., sight, sound, smell, touch).

This defense mechanism is a very functional one when a person is being abused. It allows the victim not to be present. However, depending on the severity, dissociation can be very challenging. Like other disorders, dissociation exists on a continuum and reflects a wide range of experiences and/or symptoms. At one end are the mild dissociative experiences (e.g., daydreaming). At the opposite end are the dissociative identity disorders (DID), in which a woman may have various "voices" or identities (often referred to as "alters") (Alderman and Marshall 1998).

Treatment for dissociation consists primarily of first grounding the woman, ensuring that she has the ability to self-soothe and manage stress. You will find specific grounding and self-soothing techniques throughout the curriculum.

Self-Harm

One of the most challenging behavioral symptoms experienced by some women with trauma histories is self-harming behaviors. Cutting and burning are among the most common forms of self-harm. Successful treatment of self-inflicted violence (SIV) includes teaching women new ways of coping with stressors so that underlying painful feelings can be dealt with. One of the similarities between substance abuse and self-harm is that they are both used to alter psychological or physical states. These are short-term methods of coping (Alderman 1997).

Assessing Current Trauma

In addition to past trauma, some of the participants may be experiencing abuse in current relationships. It is important that each woman in recovery be assessed for risk of current abuse. You will be teaching the women five questions to ask themselves if they are not sure if an incident was abusive.

1. Was there full consent?

2. Was there an element of betrayal, loss of trust?

3. Was there violence, pain, restriction, force, or bodily harm?

4. Did it feel like abuse to you?

5. Did you feel afraid?

It is helpful for you to know how to respond to current domestic violence. It occurs in same-sex as well as heterosexual relationships. The most important messages are that family violence is a crime, that help is available, and that you respect a woman's right to choose when she is ready and able to leave. The participants need to know that it is safe to talk with you about what they are experiencing, even if they do not feel ready to leave their relationships or take legal action. Even when a woman has a safe place to go, she may fear for her life. Often, when a woman tries to leave an abusive relationship, the violence escalates.

Here are some questions that will help you and the women in the group assess whether they have domestic violence in their lives:

1. Do you ever fear for your safety in your relationship?

2. Are you ever forced to do things against your will?

3. Have you ever been hit or threatened in the past year?

4. Have your children been hit or threatened in the past year?

5. Have you ever sustained bodily injuries, such as bruises, cuts, or broken bones?

6. Have you ever been kicked or choked?

7. Are you verbally put down, threatened, harassed; are you stalked or monitored?

If it appears a woman is in an abusive relationship, you may respond by saying:

1. I am afraid for your safety.

2. I am afraid for the safety of your children.

3. The abuse or violence will just get worse.

4. I am here for you when you are ready.

5. You deserve better than this.

6. There are safe places for you to go and people who will help you.

Local Resources

You can affirm a woman's right to decide when to leave and, at the same time, offer her a glimpse of a different life that she may create for herself. You can make available the resources to which she may turn (a shelter or safe house, legal assistance, a hot line number). It will be helpful if you have the women fill out the resource charts (p. 86) in their workbooks, should any of the women in your group need such information. It is also important to know the state and local laws regarding mandated reporting of abuse.

If it appears a woman is going to return to an abusive or violent relationship, the following statements from you may be helpful:

1. Do you feel apprehensive about returning to your relationship?

2. Is the apprehension related to a fear of being physically hurt or emotionally hurt?

3. We need to find some local resources to help you. Some possibilities are a hot line for domestic violence, a domestic violence shelter, or a mental health clinic. If we make plans about these now, you can call on them when you are ready or decide that you need them. There are also books you may want to read or other women who have gone through similar situations you may want to talk to.

Local Resources for Women in Abusive Relationships

Complete this resource list for your own area.

NAME OF PROGRAM	TYPE OF SERVICE	PHONE NUMBER

Local Resources for Women Who Have Experienced Abuse

Complete this resource list for your own area.

NAME OF PROGRAM	TYPE OF SERVICE	PHONE NUMBER

Self-Help Groups

Self-help groups are one of the resources in your community. Self-help or mutual-help groups are composed of people who voluntarily come together to discuss a common problem, often to share solutions and coping techniques. The key feature of any mutual-help group is that there is no involvement by professionals or experts who wield either authority or knowledge.

The use of mutual-help groups to recover from alcohol and other drug problems has become widespread. Moreover, the Twelve Step model, which originated in Alcoholics Anonymous (AA), is now used in more than 126 anonymous groups to deal with a host of other problems. People meeting in mutual self-help groups modeled after AA now address overeating, gambling, sexual abuse issues, and other relationship topics.

In recent years, Twelve Step programs have been critiqued in various ways. Some feminists have been concerned that the language of the Twelve Steps seems simplistic, sexist, and reductionist (Bepko 1991; Berenson 1991; Kasl 1992; Rapping 1996). Certainly, Twelve Step programs have limitations. They stress individual change as the solution and ignore social and political factors that impact women's recovery and healing. Also, much of the Twelve Step literature is thirty to sixty years old and is overtly sexist. Atheistic and agnostic women may be uncomfortable with references to a "Higher Power," even though the Twelve Steps welcome a broad range of understandings of the Higher Power, including "Goddess," "Buddha," and a "Deeper Self."

Feminists are particularly concerned about the Twelve Steps' emphasis on powerlessness. However, feminist analysis often misses the fact that the masculine "power over" is being relinquished in order to experience the feminine "power with," "power to be able"—that is, a sense of empowerment (Miller 1982). "The process of recovery from addiction is a process of recovering a different, more feminine, sense of power and will" (Berenson 1991, 74). There is also confusion between surrender and submission. "When we submit, we give in to a force that's trying to control us. When we surrender, we let go of our need to control" (Covington 1994, 48). Recovery encourages surrender and giving up the illusion of control.

Other critics say that to ask women to admit their powerlessness over alcohol/other drugs and then over persons, places, and things encourages the women to think of themselves as victims who have no control over their lives. However, this critique misses the paradox of powerlessness: By admitting her powerlessness in those aspects of her life that she cannot control, a woman accesses areas of her life in which she does have power.

Because women grow and develop in relationships and connections, and because Twelve Step programs are free and available in our communities, it makes sense to help women access them. It's best to refer a woman to a meeting you have visited or know something about. Mutual-help groups can be particularly important for women in the criminal justice system who are making the transition back into the community. Twelve Step programs also can be incorporated into community correctional settings, offering an already-existing "continuity of care."

Mutual-help groups cannot be used as substitutes for professional counseling when a female has been raped or battered or is the victim of incest. In addition, some trauma survivors are not ready for this group experience. However, as part of a multifaceted support system, mutual-help groups can be very useful for women. They can provide the kind of safe environment that is needed for trauma recovery and a growth-fostering relational context that serves women's psychological development.

Secondary Traumatization

Helping women to recover and heal can be a very rewarding experience. It can also be very demanding and challenging (Berry 2003). Secondary traumatization, or secondary traumatic stress (STS), is the language used for the reactions of counselors and facilitators who often hear very disturbing stories and constantly attend to the emotional needs of others. Burnout, compassion fatigue, and vicarious traumatization are other terms used to describe this stress that comes from helping others (Figley et al. 1995, Figley 2002). Some of the effective coping strategies that have been used for handling difficult trauma material include routine self-care: a healthy diet, regular exercise, spiritually oriented activities, and emotional support from others.

Clinical Supervision

Clinical supervision is an important part of doing trauma work. Regular, process-oriented, and psychoeducational clinical supervision needs to address the multiple issues that can arise (e.g., transference, countertransference, secondary traumatization, staff's own traumatic experiences). Regular clinical supervision where counselors can share information they have been asked to "hold" can help counselors unburden themselves. When clinical knowledge, coping skills, and support are delivered in a safe, accepting environment, this process models the therapeutic relationship.

Ethical Issues

Clients with traumatic experiences have an increased vulnerability to issues that are present in the therapeutic relationship and structure: use and abuse of power; privacy; boundary violations. Facilitators, therapists, and counselors should abide by the code of ethics that governs the policies of their agency and/or their credentials and professional affiliations.

PROGRAM INTRODUCTION

This curriculum is designed for working with women in community-based programs, private settings, or correctional settings. The suggested number of participants for a group is between six and ten women. Ideally, these would be closed groups, the women beginning and ending together. The curriculum can be adapted for larger groups and open groups if this is essential for the treatment setting. There are three primary focus areas: understanding the dynamics of violence, abuse, and trauma; understanding the impact of trauma on women's lives; and learning how to live with and to heal from trauma.

As mentioned earlier, the curriculum promotes a strength-based approach that seeks to empower women and increase their sense of self. In using this kind of model, the facilitator helps the women in the group to see the strengths and skills they already have that will aid in their healing. She looks for seeds of health and strength and mirrors this back to the women in the group. The curriculum also focuses on emotional development; dealing with expression and containment of feelings are critical parts of the trauma work.

The *Beyond Trauma* program materials consist of this facilitator's guide, a participant's workbook, two facilitator training videos, and a client video.

Using the Facilitator's Guide

- The first half of the facilitator's guide (parts one and two) gives the facilitator some background information about trauma. Having a basic understanding of the depth and complexity of the issues will help the group facilitation process.

- The second half of the facilitator's guide contains part three which includes the Session Outlines, which are similar to lesson plans. The Session Outlines are laid out in three columns: The left column indicates the topic and approximate time it takes to cover the topic; the middle column contains notes to the facilitator; and the right column includes the discussion with women.

- The curriculum has three modules (or themes) with a total of eleven sessions. The sessions may be arranged in a variety of ways; however, the curriculum is laid out in the suggested sequence.

The three modules are

a. Violence, Abuse, and Trauma

b. The Impact of Trauma on Women's Lives

c. Healing from Trauma

Your role as facilitator is to maintain the structure of the group; contain and move the group process through each session; lead by example by having appropriate boundaries and expressing and containing your feelings; and allow the women to have their own experiences of the group.

Parts four and five of the facilitator's guide provide helpful resources and references.

Session Outlines at a Glance *(see chart on pages 35–37)*

Each session is organized in the following way:

1. Goals and objectives, general topics to be covered, and materials needed (listed at the beginning of each session for the facilitator).

2. Check-in with the women in the group (at the beginning of the session).

3. Teaching component—the key topic(s) for the session are presented to enhance the women's understanding of why they felt out of control, alone, confused, disconnected from their bodies, frustrated in significant relationships, and hopeless.

4. Interactive component—the women discuss the issues, ask clarifying questions, and process the new information.

5. Experiential component—the women do exercises to try out new skills based on the information just presented in a safe, supportive environment.

6. Practice—"homework" assignments in the participant's workbooks give the women an opportunity to practice the new skills they have learned.

7. Integration—an opportunity to explore the impact of the new learning/ behavior.

8. Closure includes a reflection and sometimes a relaxation exercise.

Session Outlines at a Glance

MODULE	SESSION	DESCRIPTION	MATERIALS NEEDED
A: **Violence, Abuse, and Trauma**			
	1	**The Connections between Violence, Abuse, and Trauma**	• Name tags • Participant's workbook • Easel pad, felt pens, masking tape, crayons, colored pencils • Cassette or CD player and relaxing music • Tissues • VCR and monitor • Client video
	2	**Power and Abuse**	• Easel pad, felt pens, masking tape • *Circle of Stones* (Duerk 1993) *(optional)* • Participant's workbook • Cassette or CD player and relaxing music • Tissues • VCR and monitor • Client video
B: **The Impact of Trauma on Women's Lives**			
	3	**Reactions to Trauma**	• Easel pad, felt pens, masking tape • Small bags with various items • Cassette or CD player and relaxing music • Tissues • VCR and monitor • Participant's workbook • Client video

MODULE	SESSION	DESCRIPTION	MATERIALS NEEDED
	4	**How Trauma Impacts Our Lives**	• Easel pad, felt pens, masking tape • Participant's workbook • Cassette or CD player and relaxing music • Magazines for collage exercise • A piece of poster board for each participant • Glue sticks and scissors for group to share • Tissues
C: Healing from Trauma			
	5	**The Addiction and Trauma Connection: Spirals of Recovery and Healing**	• Easel pad, felt pens, masking tape, crayons • Participant's workbook • Cassette or CD player and relaxing music • VCR and monitor • Tissues • Client video
	6	**Grounding and Self-Soothing**	• Easel pad, felt pens, masking tape • Cassette or CD player and relaxing music • Participant's workbook • Tissues
	7	**Abuse and the Family**	• Easel pad, felt pens, masking tape • Participant's workbook • Cassette or CD player and relaxing music • VCR and monitor • Tissues • Client video

MODULE	SESSION	DESCRIPTION	MATERIALS NEEDED
	8	**Mind and Body Connection**	• Easel pad, felt pens, masking tape, crayons or colored pencils • Participant's workbook • Cassette or CD player and relaxing music • Tissues • Large sheets of butcher paper *(optional)*
	9	**The World of Feelings**	• Easel pad, felt pens, masking tape, crayons or colored pencils • Cassette or CD player and relaxing music • Tissues • Participant's workbook
	10	**Healthy Relationships: Wheel of Love**	• Easel pad, felt pens, masking tape • Participant's workbook • Cassette or CD player and relaxing music • VCR and monitor • Magazines for collage exercise • A piece of poster board for each participant • Glue sticks and scissors for group to share • Tissues • Client video
	11	**Endings and Beginnings**	• Pretty piece of fabric, scarf, or tablecloth • Meaningful object *(optional)* • Participant's workbook • Easel pad, felt pens, masking tape • Cassette or CD player and relaxing music • Tissues

Examples are given throughout the curriculum. These examples of typical responses from women are included so the facilitator has a sense of what to expect from the exercise or question she is posing. Additionally, the examples may be useful prompts for the facilitator to stimulate further discussion among the participants.

- Each individual or small-group activity is listed as an exercise. General discussion questions to the full group are not listed as exercises.

- Adult learning theory suggests that for maximum attention and retention, "nonlecture" activities be interjected approximately every seven to ten minutes. Therefore, the curriculum is designed to be interactive, with facilitator-generated exercises and questions for participants. Keep in mind that people learn in different ways. People need to hear, see (via a role model), and try out (role-play) new ideas and concepts.

- The facilitator is encouraged to enhance the learning experience by tailoring information, data, and exercises to the conditions and needs of the participants. This includes cultural issues, educational levels and literacy, and unique concerns of criminal justice settings.

What Makes a Good Facilitator?

The following qualities in a facilitator will help to ensure a positive group experience:

1. trustworthy

2. credible

3. available

4. reliable, consistent

5. hopeful

6. warm, compassionate

7. emotionally mature

8. healthy boundaries, respects confidentiality

9. committed to and interested in women's issues

10. sensitive and responsive to multicultural issues

11. appropriate gender—a female should facilitate the all-female groups

12. if a trauma survivor, confident that she is at a place in her own recovery that will allow for healthy and positive outcomes for herself and the women in the group

13. content expert

14. skilled as a facilitator

There are many unique challenges to being a facilitator in a criminal justice setting (confidentiality, support, group space, comfort, security, etc.). It is particularly important in this setting for the facilitator to provide confidentiality and emotional safety, as well as be an advocate for the women and the group. Often there is a "culture clash" in criminal justice settings. Historically, the criminal justice system has been based on a control model while the treatment field is based on a change model. Some treatment providers struggle to work in a setting that feels unsupportive.

Prior to the Session

The following sections on basic group facilitation are designed for new facilitators and provide a review for those with experience.

- Before beginning the group, it is suggested that facilitators allow six to eight hours for reading and comprehending the curriculum materials. It is also useful to review the current session materials again right before the session. This is necessary in order for the facilitator to feel comfortable with and absorb the information. Facilitators will want to be able to present the materials by just referring to their notes and not "reading" them.

- Help the women find a support person (friend, mental health provider) to be available for them between sessions. This may be another challenge in a criminal justice setting, where support may not be readily available.

- Be sure all equipment (e.g., easel pad, cassette or CD player) is available in advance and in the session room.

- Check to be sure the "logistics" are arranged (e.g., special needs, transportation, room, chairs, name tags, doors unlocked). For example, you might need to find a secure place for the women's workbooks if you work in a correctional setting.

- Room size is important. The room should be large enough to accommodate the group comfortably; participants should have easy access in and out of their chairs without disturbing others, and not be too cramped. Rooms too large can make the setting cold and impersonal.

- Good ventilation and room temperature is important for an effective and comfortable group environment. The room should have windows and/or natural light.

- The physical environment in your group meeting room is important. Ideally, you could create a soothing, healing atmosphere in the room by providing a flower or plant; calm, relaxing music; soft, warm lighting (nonglaring, nonfluorescent); comfortable chairs already arranged so there is not chaos when the women enter the room; drinking water nearby; a box of tissues; and the like. The room should be free from distractions created by others outside the room. Likewise, the participants should not be visible to others outside the room. If the meetings are at night, there should be adequate lighting outside the meeting room and in the parking lot. Establishing this kind of group atmosphere may be challenging in criminal justice settings.

- Make sure rest rooms are located nearby and easily accessible.

- Good acoustics facilitate good communication. If the room is too large or not soundproof to outside noises, it may not be an effective session location. Noise distractions can be disruptive; participants may fear others outside can hear and breach confidentiality.

- Be sure the group room meets the Americans with Disabilities Act (ADA) standards and accommodates any special needs of participants and facilitators.

- Arrive at the group room at least ten minutes before the session begins. This allows time for you to be sure that all equipment is there and functioning and that the chairs are in a circle. Circular settings foster a sense of respect and equality, as well as allow each woman to make eye contact with others in the group.

Knowing the Women in the Group

- Know something about the women in your group. This is not only respectful but will help your facilitation. Find out who they are, what they want to know and learn, and what their level of experience, their current emotional state, their level of functioning, and any particular group dynamics are. You may wish to develop a questionnaire to help gather this information before the first session. Understand and learn as much as you can ahead of time about the issues, concerns, and demographic profiles of the women in the group. These could include issues of race, class, and culture. Time is also set aside during the session itself to discuss this information with participants.

- Women need enough mental health and cognitive functioning to participate in the exercises and discussions. Women who have certain mental illnesses or disabilities that may prevent them from participating need to have a group modified for them.

- Women may be either self-referred or recommended by a counselor. It is important to clarify this when starting a group. Sometimes a woman who has been referred by a counselor may feel resentful about attending. This may help to assess motivation of the group members. Acknowledging that there will be benefits to each woman in the group for attending and expressing in a personal way that you are pleased that they are going to be part of the group may be helpful.

Cofacilitating

- This curriculum is designed to be led by one facilitator. However, you may find you prefer to facilitate with another person. If so, spend some time in advance talking with the other facilitator regarding how to divide up the sections, facilitating methods and styles of delivery, as well as "sharing the stage."

1. Review goals and procedures for sessions.

2. Identify who will lead discussions.

3. Have a backup plan in case a facilitator is unable to do the session.

4. Discuss how the cofacilitators will interact. For example, are both facilitators comfortable if the other facilitator interjects examples or ideas?

- At the end of each session, facilitators should debrief the session and review any feedback:

  1. Discuss the group process.

  2. Review and discuss participants' feedback, reactions, and responses.

  3. Discuss how each woman in the group is doing and plan for any special attention that might be needed to get group members to connect with each other. If you encourage the women to connect with each other between sessions, you will help build strong networks of caring women.

- Each facilitator needs to determine ahead of time how she will handle any one-on-one time with individual group members between sessions.

Tips on Running a Group

Reliability

- Facilitators need to commit to attending each session to (1) build trust, (2) show that they are committed to the group, (3) maintain a sense of consistency/continuity that plays a part in creating safety.

- It is also important as a facilitator to be emotionally constant for the women in the group.

- Start on time and end on time.

Style

- Being culturally sensitive and using culturally relevant examples is important throughout the curriculum. Difference in age, sexual orientation, religion, race, class, disability, culture, and ethnicity can influence women's levels of comfort with the issues discussed in this program.

- Be supportive and nonjudgmental, and give support to participants: "That's a good question. I am glad you raised that."

- Keep language simple and clear, and avoid jargon. If acronyms or abbreviations are used, explain what they mean (*DSM-IV-TR,* DOC, etc.).

- Summarize individual or group feelings regularly. The facilitator might want to summarize common themes that have evolved throughout the group session.

- Be conscious of group trust and confidentiality. The facilitator needs to watch interactions that have the potential to impact the cohesiveness of the group. This might include competition among members, absenteeism, silence, nonparticipation, subgrouping, a breach of confidentiality, and more. Verbally check in with the group regarding these issues (e.g., ask them, "What does the silence mean?").

- Set standards for an acceptable way of relating with others (e.g., no physical or verbal abuse, no interrupting, no name-calling).

Group Interaction

- To minimize disruption to group communication, ask participants in community-based settings to turn off the ringers on their pagers and cellular phones (suggest using less disruptive notification systems such as vibration, text messaging, or digital display if communication is necessary).

- Encourage the women to speak about their personal experiences, not give generalizations or abstractions, while keeping the pace moving along. At the same time, women get to set their own limits with respect to self-disclosure. This helps to create safety. Sharing personal experiences increases connection and closeness with others. It also enables the women to learn from one another's experiences.

- Encourage participation by all women, yet respect their own comfort levels, need for contemplation, and healing. It is important to understand a woman's resilience as well as her struggles with a painful event. Disclosing and listening to the stories of other women may be upsetting for her. Some group members may feel too vulnerable and at risk to share personal information. A woman who has experienced trauma will need enough time to observe and assess the facilitator's and other group members' abilities to create an environment in which she can feel safe.

- The process of retelling a trauma may restimulate the trauma memories. Even though this may stir up physiological distress, the goal is to focus on how the traumatic experiences have impacted women's minds, bodies, and spirits and not to uncover or retrieve traumatic memories. If women retell the story of their trauma, the facilitator needs to emphasize strengths, coping capabilities, and resilience. Focusing on women's personal strengths rather than solely on the trauma pain is more helpful in this stage of the healing process. In general, it is more useful to focus on understanding the impact of the memories of the trauma, to connect with other survivors, and to learn new, healthy coping strategies.

- Be aware that too much disclosure on the facilitator's part may be inappropriate and derail the group process. It is also detrimental to use the group as a sounding board for your personal concerns. If you are considering self-disclosing, always ask yourself, "What would be most helpful for the women in the group?" Remember, in a support group, the important discoveries will come from the group members. Your self-disclosure should be kept at a minimum, except when you are sharing at the beginning of session 1.

- Some facilitators may intervene during a conflict between group members because of their own discomfort rather than allowing the women to explore the depths of the issue at hand. Be sure you understand the motivation behind your actions. If you are acting on an impulse, it is more likely to be about you than the group process.

- Many of these topics are emotionally draining, even for the facilitator. Clinical supervision for a facilitator is very important. Share with a colleague what topics impact you personally—this is especially important for facilitators who are also survivors of abuse. If you feel overwhelmed, seek help from a colleague or other professional.

- It is important that the facilitator be a woman. Her role is that of a guide on a journey seen through the eyes of women. Many of the issues addressed in this curriculum are common to all women.

- Keep the group focused on the relevant topics in the curriculum.

- Confidentiality is a value that must be adhered to by the facilitator as well as the group members. There are two exceptions: (1) you may communicate with treatment team members as part of a woman's ongoing care, or (2) you may break confidentiality when someone's personal safety or the safety of others is at stake.

- Ask the women to listen to each other attentively without interrupting. Each woman has an important experience to relate, which should not be judged or challenged. All feelings are real for the person feeling them. No one should be told how to feel.

- Strive for complete honesty. Honesty need not be in conflict with privacy or protecting the feelings of others. Remind yourself and the women in the group that honesty without sensitivity can hurt feelings, decrease connection, and appear mean-spirited.

- Encourage the women to share all comments, questions, and opinions with the group. This may help others with the same issue. Side conversations can alienate and divide group members.

- Make no assumptions about the literacy level of group members. Allow them to draw instead of writing if reading and writing are difficult for them, or have women pair up with others who can read and do assignments. Women often have shame regarding their writing skills and sometimes drop out of a group because of it. Explain words, concepts, and homework assignments carefully. Do not assume that a person's level of literacy equates with her level of intelligence.

- Discussing common issues and problems can help women alleviate feelings of isolation. Explore ideas about how to make personal life changes. Explore what keeps each woman from making personal changes and what kind of support she needs from the group or others.

- When appropriate, inject humor and lightness into the conversation. If everything is intense and serious, group members may become too overwhelmed.

Cultural Awareness

- Remember that race, ethnicity, and gender are not mutually exclusive. Together they are part of the complex lens through which many women see and experience the world they live in. Simply discussing issues related to women, generically, does not recognize the importance of the racial and/or ethnic identities of the women in the group.

- Help women see the social/cultural context for these issues. The traumas and burdens each woman has faced may be the result of being female, poor, a woman of color, and so on. Awareness of this can help reduce the personal shame or blame she may feel.

- Valuing diversity not only works to dismantle various negative stereotypes about race, ethnicity, and culture; it may also work to counter the stereotypes that individual women in the group may have internalized in their lives.

- Encourage the women to get involved in some sort of social action, such as letter writing, lobbying, political action, or volunteering in the community to fight injustices and create change in their lives and the lives of others.

Managing Challenging Group Members

- During the group session, manage the discussion and do not let one or two people dominate. Start a session by saying, "I would like to start this discussion by inviting people who have not spoken to give us their thoughts and feelings." It is important that different viewpoints get expressed. Possible responses to difficult, controlling, or domineering people include

  a. Politely interrupt them with a statement such as "Can we put that on the back burner for the moment and return to it later?" or "If it is all right, I would like to ask if we can discuss that after the session. There's another important point we still need to discuss, and we are running a little short of time."

  b. You can also jump in at a pause with "That is a good point. Have others felt this way?" or redirect the conversation: "We have had several comments in support of this idea; are there different thoughts or feelings about this?" This approach brings the focus back to the group as a whole and encourages others to speak.

- A good facilitator allows everyone a chance to speak and facilitates opportunities for less vocal people in the circle to be heard. If people do not participate in discussions or appear to have their minds elsewhere, you may want to call on them by name to give an answer, share an opinion, or recount an experience. Always give them the option not to speak if they prefer not to. Always praise the person for responding.

- If a discussion escalates and becomes highly emotional, divert the conversation away from the people participating before it gets out of hand. "I think we all know how Latisha and Susanne feel about this. Now, does anyone else have a comment?" Or, validate their feelings or emotional reactions by saying something such as, "Clearly this is a very emotional and difficult issue with differing viewpoints." Intense emotions can also be a good indicator of major issues just underneath the surface. You may want to give extra time for discussion to see if some clarity or understanding can come out of it.

- As you go along, register steps of agreement and disagreement with participants. Say, "Am I correct in assuming we all agree (or disagree) on this point?" or "You may simply agree to disagree on certain issues since each person is unique."

- If you need to control the person who "knows it all," acknowledge the person's contribution and then ask others in the group for their opinion of the person's statement.

- When a discussion gets off track, say: "Your point is an interesting one, but it is a little different from the main issues here; perhaps we can address your issues after the session," or "We will be talking about that later in session X. Your points are very interesting; could you hold those thoughts until we get to that module?"

- If a person speaks in broad generalizations, ask, "Can you give us a specific example on that point?" or "Your general idea is a good one, but I wonder if we can make it even more concrete. Does anyone know of a situation where . . . ?"

- If a person in the group states something that is incorrect (yet no one addresses the misinformation), avoid direct or public criticism. You can graciously correct the information or use indirect methods to set the record straight, such as analyzing a similar situation where the correct information is given. You may also want to talk to the person after the session and share the correct information.

- If a person is difficult in a group session, next time be sure to sit next to her. This proximity of the facilitator can often help mediate difficulties.

- Generally, try not to interrupt participants. Be respectful and listen. Be open yet firm and manage the discussion, keeping in mind what is best for the whole group.

Answering Questions

- Anticipate the types of questions women might ask and plan how to handle them. As you get ready for the session, consider the questions you are most likely to get and think about your answers. You can also use these questions to stimulate group discussions throughout your session. Make sure your questions are designed to get thoughtful reactions to specific points. Do not ask questions that can be answered by a "yes" or "no" response. Open-ended questions generate better participation.

- Questions from participants are a good indication of the level of their awareness, attention, and interest in the subject. Questions have value in helping you to clarify, modify, or fortify points or to test an idea for its potential. Remember that answering a question is impromptu. Pause if you need to, relax, maintain your poise, keep your answers short and to the point, and give the short answer first (e.g., yes or no); then explain why.

- Some questions involving women's specific situations may border on giving legal advice (e.g., can I sue the perpetrator?). Be clear about what questions are legal matters and when it is more appropriate to refer the question to legal aid or a lawyer.

- If you do not know the answer to a question, acknowledge that fact; then offer to find the information. Not all questions have to be answered. Sometimes the most effective response is one that allows the participants to keep thinking about the issue or concern.

- After you answer a question from a woman, ask her, "Does that answer your question?" "Do you agree?" or "Has that been your experience as well?"

- Rephrase questions that are unclear or rambling.

- Avoid a one-to-one conversation or argument with a participant. Many women have come from a harsh environment, and the group is one place they should feel safe and supported.

- The curriculum includes data and numbers that were current at the time of this printing. You are encouraged to update or find local statistics before a session.

Special Considerations for Criminal Justice Settings

As previously mentioned, holding a group in a criminal justice setting has its own unique challenges. The facilitator needs to think through the following issues before the sessions begin (Bloom, Owen, and Covington 2003). Some challenges include

- space and setting (Can chairs be moved in a circle? Is music allowed? Is privacy allowed or must correctional staff be present? Are there other security issues that affect the setting and environment you are trying to create?)

- confidentiality (Is confidentiality more difficult to ensure in a setting where security is prioritized and trust is not the norm?)

- interruptions (These may include the offender "count," observations by correctional officers, inflexible times women are called out for court or medication, special security issues.)

- attitudes of group members (Are some mandated to be there? Are women resistant to being there? Are women going to group only because they do not want to be somewhere else?)

- materials/workbooks (Are women allowed to have materials in their cells? Do women have the time and permission to do the activities in their setting?)

- support for facilitator (The correctional environment can be harsh for the facilitator as well as for the women. Getting support from someone within the institution or correctional setting can help the facilitator navigate the system more easily as well as provide an emotional sounding board for her concerns.)

- standard operating practices may traumatize and/or retraumatize women (searches, restraints, isolation).

Group Process

- The length of each session is one hour, thirty minutes.

- It is important to create safety in the group, both external safety and internal safety. The group setting needs to be free from physical and emotional discomfort and fear. Many of the women in the group have never felt safe because others betrayed their safety. These women spend a great deal of energy trying to keep themselves safe or being anxious when they do not feel safe. Setting limits, ground rules, and boundaries can help women feel safe.

- The emotional environment is also critical to the success of the session and the comfort of the group members. Develop trust and confidentiality in these therapeutic group settings. As facilitator, you can ensure that group members feel there is mutual caring and input, rather than an authoritarian or judgmental setting. Judith Herman calls trauma "the disease of disconnection" (1992). A group, therefore, can help establish connection and healing. Encourage mutual, respectful, and compassionate connections among the women.

- Group agreements or ground rules are crucial to the smooth running of a group. Basic guidelines for group participation and confidentiality need to be discussed early on with all women in the group. Defining the agreements right from the start serves to create a safe group culture. This provides the foundation for women to feel comfortable sharing their feelings, asking questions, and fully engaging with the others and with the materials.

  Group agreements should be clear, short, simple, and direct. Confidentiality, nonviolence, and not coming to group under the influence of alcohol or other drugs are three agreements that are nonnegotiable. Have the group come up with other rules and do your best to get group consensus. Sample agreements might include the following:

  1. Group members need to honor each other's confidentiality. What is said in this room stays in this room.

     You might want to ask group members: "What does confidentiality mean to you? What happens when it is violated? How does that feel? What do you want to do, as a group, to maintain confidentiality?" As mentioned earlier, in criminal justice settings confidentiality can be particularly complicated. Discussing specifics about crimes may impact their sentencing, probation, or parole.

  2. Violence and aggressive behavior is not permitted. No physical, emotional, or verbal abuse will be tolerated in the group.

3. Sessions will start on time and end on time.

4. Regular attendance and participation is important for everyone in the group.

   Making the commitment to attend is something that the women are doing for themselves as well as for the group as a whole. Their contributions are greatly valued. In criminal justice settings, the fact that women may be court-ordered to attend may change the atmosphere, and it may be necessary to emphasize the importance of them being there in a different way. Tell group members that although they may have been court-ordered, if they keep an open mind, the group may be helpful to them.

   Group members should contact the facilitator if they are unable to attend a session. If someone misses a session, she needs to complete the homework and then review the information from the session with the facilitator.

5. Contact with other group members outside the regular group session is permitted.

6. Share the floor with others—everyone in the group should have the time to talk and share what is on her mind.

7. No smoking in the group sessions.

8. Do not come to the group session under the influence of drugs or alcohol.

9. Having feelings is okay. Crying in the group is okay. Laughing is okay. Getting angry is okay. Being abusive to another group member is not okay.

10. Women in the group are always free to "pass" when asked a question or asked to do an exercise that requires participation. Note that it is important for the facilitator to take time after the group to privately ask the woman why she passed. Often, those who do not speak have a great deal to say but may not feel comfortable sharing in a group setting. Find out how you may be able to assist the women in feeling safe enough to share.

- Empower the women in the group. The facilitator can point out and emphasize the women's strengths. She can encourage women to make conscious decisions. She can also help women to take ownership of their feelings and act out their feelings in appropriate ways, rather than suppressing them or being consumed by them. Encourage social action as part of the healing process.

- The curriculum uses "guided imagery," or visualizations, in several sessions. The facilitator should become familiar and comfortable with this therapeutic approach. The facilitator's relaxed style and ease in explaining the visualization, often developed through practice, is helpful in making the women feel relaxed. This safe, serene, yet purposefully guided approach maximizes their experience.

  The goal of guided imagery is to allow women the opportunity to visualize or imagine a scenario different from their own reality. It can be an opportunity for them to safely see or try out behaviors in a safe structure. It allows them to break through boundaries or barriers that may be hindering their healing process. It opens up their world to possibilities.

  It is important in a visualization exercise to slowly bring the women out of the experience and into the here and now. Once you have finished the visualization and have had the women open their eyes, it is important to indicate the visualization has ended. For some trauma survivors, closing their eyes for an exercise can be very difficult. Women with PTSD and other anxiety disorders can develop increased anxiousness. They may need to keep their eyes open until there is a deeper sense of safety and trust.

- Begin each group with some quiet time and a brief check-in. Close each group with time to reflect on what has been covered. Remind the group of the confidentiality commitment agreed to by all the group members. Opening and closing activities also help ground the women and make them feel present.

- Ideally, the group should be closed to new members after the first session so that the entire group begins and ends together. This helps establish connection with other group members. The material in this curriculum builds from session to session, and the first session lays the foundation for trust among the group members. Once the program is completed, it may be decided (depending on your setting and if the group members so desire) to let the group continue as an ongoing support group. The curriculum can also run as an open group if the setting requires an open group process.

❧ Conclusion ❧

You have just finished reading the introduction to *Beyond Trauma,* which was designed to give you some background information about the process and treatment of trauma in women's lives. You have also received details about the curriculum itself, as well as basic information on group facilitation. For some of you this material was new and for others it was a review.

The next section of the facilitator's guide is Session Outlines, similar to lesson plans. These outlines create the structure and content of the program. They also provide the process that the women will experience.

Although training in the use of the curriculum is available, the facilitators guide and videos are designed to provide self-instruction. You will find that the combination of reading the materials (including the participant's workbook) and viewing the two facilitator's videos before you start the process will be very helpful. The videos elaborate on the information in the facilitator's guide by providing additional explanations, examples, and demonstrations of many of the exercises.

Again, thank you for your commitment to helping women grow and heal.

SESSION OUTLINES (MODULES)

MODULE A

Violence, Abuse, and Trauma

Session 1

The Connections between Violence, Abuse, and Trauma

Session 2

Power and Abuse

The Connections between Violence, Abuse, and Trauma

▧ Time

1 hour 30 minutes

▧ Session Goal

Women will understand the connection between violence, abuse, and trauma.

▧ Participant Learning Objectives

1. To understand the definition of trauma
2. To understand the prevalence of trauma
3. To describe examples of traumatic events in a woman's life
4. To become familiar with the different responses to trauma

▧ Session Overview

- Welcome, Goals, Introductions, Group Agreements, Logistics
- Definition of *Trauma*
- Examples of Traumatic Events
- How Often Trauma Occurs
- Substance Abuse and Trauma
- Gender Differences with Violence and Abuse
- Different Responses to Trauma
- *Exercise: Creating Safety*
- *Reflection and Homework*

▧ Materials and Equipment Needed

- Name tags
- Participant's workbook
- Easel pad, felt pens, masking tape, crayons, colored pencils
- Cassette or CD player and relaxing music
- Tissues
- VCR and monitor
- *Beyond Trauma* client video

The Connections between Violence, Abuse, and Trauma

TIME & TOPIC	FACILITATOR NOTES	DISCUSSION WITH WOMEN
10 min. **Welcome, introduction, and goals for the group**	*Introduce yourself, describe your background and your interest in working with women and trauma, and also describe your role as the facilitator.* *Prepare for each session ahead of time so you do not need to read the "Discussion with Women" word for word.* *Remember, these are some of the things that you are responsible for:* • *beginning and ending on time* • *maintaining structure of the group* • *moving the group through the content of each session* • *leading by example by having appropriate boundaries and containing your feelings* • *allowing each woman to have her own experience of the group* *This is your first opportunity to establish trust, credibility, and a connection with the women in the group.*	Welcome, and I am glad you are here. My name is _____ , and I will be the facilitator for the group. This group is designed to help you gain insight and skills in order to better manage the difficult experience of dealing with the effects of trauma in your life. Traumatic experiences can cause distress in the mind, the body, and the spirit. Understanding and dealing with the effects of trauma in your life will help you understand more about yourself and help you discover how to have a healthy relationship with yourself and with others. We will be meeting for eleven sessions and covering a variety of topics that are important in our lives. For the period of time that we meet, each of you will have the opportunity to share feelings and experiences that are unique to you. The stories and the wisdom that you bring to the rest of the group are invaluable. Each and every one of you will contribute greatly to making the collective group a rich and supportive environment. Here you will find commonalities and differences, but most important, a space to share your voice, to be heard, and to be supported by other women. Each session will run for one hour and thirty minutes without a break. If you look at the table of contents in your workbook (page iii), you will see an outline of all the sessions and topics we will be covering in

TIME & TOPIC	FACILITATOR NOTES	DISCUSSION WITH WOMEN
		our group. We will be using the workbooks both in the sessions and for homework. It is important to look at the links between violence, abuse, and trauma while also looking at the role power plays in the continuation of abuse that women face in their lives. To help us understand the impact that trauma has on our lives, we will discuss the physical, mental, emotional, and social effects of trauma. We will do this in part by looking at two spirals: (1) addiction and recovery, and (2) trauma and healing. We will learn some techniques that you can use in your day-to-day lives that will help you ground and soothe yourself. These techniques may help you in your journey as you go through the process of learning to cope with the effects of trauma. Each session will begin with a quiet time and check-in with everyone and end with a reflection on what we have shared and learned from one another.
2 min. **Quiet time**	*You may want to play some soft music during this quiet time.*	Let us take a few minutes of quiet time so each of us can have a moment to unwind, get rid of stresses from the day, and become present in the group. Let us be silent for a minute or two to relax and focus on where we are now.
20 min. **Why we are here and overview of trauma**		Personal growth, recovery, and healing are a lifelong journey. The trauma we have experienced may always be with us at some level. If we take the risk of learning about trauma and give ourselves the opportunity to explore the process of healing, we can

TIME & TOPIC	FACILITATOR NOTES	DISCUSSION WITH WOMEN
		grow and cope and live happy and healthy lives after a traumatic experience. Trauma can impact our lives in many ways. • Impacts inner self: It can impact our inner lives—our thoughts, feelings, beliefs, values. For example, some women believe that "you can't trust anyone," and "the world is a very unsafe place." • Impacts outer self: It can impact our outer lives—our outer life is our relationships and behavior. Many women who have experienced trauma struggle with their relationships—families, friends, sexual relationships. For example, parenting is a relationship that can become even more complicated by the experience of trauma. Some women who have experienced childhood abuse may be triggered back to their abuse experience by their own child. The risk for this happening is greatest when a woman's child becomes the age she was when the abuse first occurred. Another part of our outer self is our behavior. Some women become numb, isolated, and asexual. For other women, their behavior is at the opposite end of the continuum. They may become agitated, loud, and often hypersexual. A major part of the healing process is becoming congruent. This means having the inner self (thoughts, feelings, beliefs) connected to, and consistent with, the outer self (behavior and relationships). For example, does your face (outer self) reflect how you are feeling (inner self)? Here are some of the questions that women who have experienced trauma often struggle with:

TIME & TOPIC	FACILITATOR NOTES	DISCUSSION WITH WOMEN
		• Why did this happen to me? • What did I do wrong? • Why do I feel so ashamed? • Why did people hurt me? • Why is life such a struggle? • What do I do now? As one woman described her experience: "I often feel really ashamed and depressed about all of the abuse I have seen and experienced and wonder if I will ever be able to be happy. The strange thing is I am so good at putting on a smile when I see people. Even when people could see the bruises, I would pretend like nothing was happening, even though I knew that they knew. Really, on the inside I just wanted to cry or talk about it, but I was too afraid—it made me feel crazy, like I was living in two different worlds or something." This group provides a safe space to explore your thoughts and feelings. You may find that many of the questions you have are similar to those of other women in the group. The healing journey can be challenging, but it is also filled with hope.
Group participant introductions	*Facilitators familiar with the* Helping Women Recover *curriculum (Covington 1999) may want to substitute the "people, events, experiences" exercise for introductions.*	We will get to know each other pretty well over the next few weeks/months. So, I would like to begin by having each of you introduce yourself. Please share your name and any other information you would like to share, such as little-known facts about yourself that are not visible by looking at you (e.g., you are a mother, a sister, a recovering alcoholic; you just finished school; you are happy to be here in the group; you have a new puppy).

TIME & TOPIC	FACILITATOR NOTES	DISCUSSION WITH WOMEN
Group agreements	*Generate the group agreements from participants. Write the ideas on the easel pad and tape the list onto the wall. Display it on the wall at each session.* *Confidentiality, no physical or emotional abuse, and not attending group sessions under the influence of alcohol or other drugs must be three of the group agreements.* *Examples of other group agreements are listed at right.*	Now that we have met each other, it's time to come up with a set of agreements that will give shape to the group process. These are agreements that you feel are important to make with one another to ensure that the group remains a safe and supportive space for each of you. 1. Group members need to honor each other's confidentiality. What is said in this room stays in this room. 2. Sessions will start on time and end on time. 3. Group members need to respect one another. 4. Regular group attendance is important. Group members need to establish a policy for missed meetings, such as group members should contact the facilitator if they are unable to attend a session, how the work missed in a session can be made up, etc. 5. Contact with other group members outside the regular group session is permitted. 6. Share the time with others—everyone in the group should have the time to contribute and share the experience. 7. No smoking in the group sessions. 8. No eating and drinking in the group sessions. My role as the facilitator is to support and guide the group through the material in the curriculum. We will talk a great deal about creating safety in the group and in other aspects of our lives. In the group, this means that we will focus on how trauma impacts us in the present and how we can take care of ourselves now and in the future.

TIME & TOPIC	FACILITATOR NOTES	DISCUSSION WITH WOMEN
Support and Logistics	*Discuss who will be available between group sessions if the women have questions or concerns. This is particularly important if you are running this group in an outpatient setting or a correctional facility.* *Additionally, provide information on the following things:* • *location of bathrooms* • *location of pay phones* • *no ringers on cell phones, pagers, etc. on during sessions* • *parking or public transportation issues*	
30 min. **Definition of *trauma***	*Have women share their thoughts about what the word* trauma *means. Write responses on the easel pad.*	What is trauma? Trauma is any stressor that occurs in a sudden and forceful way and is experienced as overwhelming. However, trauma and stress are not the same thing. Certainly, all traumatic events are stressful, but not all stressful events are traumatic. Removing the causes of stress can reverse the symptoms of stress. The symptoms of trauma must be addressed differently because it has a deeper and more far-reaching impact. Women who have experienced traumatic events describe feelings of intense fear, helplessness, or horror. These are normal reactions to abnormal or extreme situations.

TIME & TOPIC	FACILITATOR NOTES	DISCUSSION WITH WOMEN
		We know that no two people experience trauma in the same way. Many things influence how a woman responds to a traumatic event: her age, history with other trauma, family dynamics, support systems, and more. We know that what may be a traumatic event for one person may not be for another. One woman may feel her situation was life threatening—making her feel vulnerable and afraid. Another woman may experience that same kind of situation differently. It is important to remember that each woman's experience and her feelings surrounding that experience need to be honored.

Understanding trauma and that we respond to it differently will help us be supportive and nonjudgmental toward each other. Women need support to heal from trauma. Part of the process in healing from trauma is developing connection and support with others. |
| **Video:** *Beyond Trauma*

 Client video

 • INTRODUCTION
 • WHAT IS TRAUMA?
 • GROUP COMMENTS | *Show video: Segment 1.* | |
| **Examples of traumatic events** | *Discuss and write responses on the easel pad. Fill in what women miss with the examples listed at right.* | What are some examples of traumatic events?

 Trauma can take many forms: emotional, sexual, or physical abuse; extremely painful and frightening medical procedures; catastrophic injuries and illnesses; rape or assault; muggings; domestic violence; burglary; witnessing murder; automobile accidents; abandonment (especially for small children); culturally bound, intergenerational |

TIME & TOPIC	FACILITATOR NOTES	DISCUSSION WITH WOMEN
		(e.g., Native Americans); immigration; natural disasters (hurricanes, earthquakes, tornadoes, fires, floods, volcanoes); terrorism (such as September 11, 2001); witnessing violence (such as a parent harming another parent); loss of a loved one and severe bereavements (including a pet); combat/war; torture; kidnapping; etc.
		Of all these forms of trauma, women are at greater risk of interpersonal violence than men.
		Stigmatization (e.g., that of incarcerated women, women of color, poor women, lesbians, transgendered women) is another dynamic that can cause trauma in a woman's life. Let me read an excerpt written by a noted black writer to help us understand how stigmatization can be traumatizing. This is from Audre Lorde's *Sister Outsider*.
	(Reprinted with permission from *Sister Outsider* by Audre Lorde. Copyright ©1984 by Audre Lorde, The Crossing Press, a division of Ten Speed Press, Berkeley, CA, 94707, www.tenspeed.com)	The AA subway train to Harlem. I clutched my mother's sleeve, her arms full of shopping bags, Christmas-heavy. The wet smell of winter clothes, the train's lurching. My mother spots an almost seat, pushes my little snow-suited body down. On one side of me a man reading a paper. On the other, a woman in a fur hat staring at me. Her mouth twitches as she stares and then her gaze drops down, pulling mine with it. Her leather-gloved hand plucks at the line where my new blue snow pants and her sleek fur coat meet. She jerks her coat closer to her. I look. I do not see whatever terrible thing she is seeing on the seat between us—probably a roach. But she has communicated her horror to me. It must be something very bad from the way she is looking, so I pull my snowsuit closer

TIME & TOPIC	FACILITATOR NOTES	DISCUSSION WITH WOMEN
		to me away from it, too. When I look up, the woman is still staring at me, her nose holes and eyes huge. And suddenly I realize there is nothing crawling up the seat between us; it is me she doesn't want her coat to touch. The fur brushes past my face as she stands with a shudder and holds on to a strap in the speeding train. Born and bred a New York City child, I quickly slide over to make room for my mother to sit down. No word has been spoken. I'm afraid to say anything to my mother because I don't know what I've done. I look at the sides of my snow pants, secretly. Is there something on them? Something's going on here I do not understand, but I will never forget it. Her eyes. The flared nostrils. The hate.
		As I read this story, and earlier gave examples of types of traumatic situations, you may have noticed your own body's response to hearing the words—you may have experienced tingling, muscles tightening or loosening, increased or decreased heart rate, numbness, paralysis, temperature changes, different colors or shapes appearing in your inner field of vision, thoughts or emotions, or fleeting images— or maybe you felt nothing in your body. Pay attention to these things that occur automatically or almost unconsciously. We will be addressing these feelings by becoming aware of them and then learning strategies for coping with these feelings.
	Discuss.	What were some of your thoughts and feelings as I read this? Have you experienced or observed similar situations?

TIME & TOPIC	FACILITATOR NOTES	DISCUSSION WITH WOMEN
How often trauma occurs	*Read the statistics so that the women get a sense of the magnitude of the problem.* *After reading the statistics, check in with the women. Ask them if they had trouble concentrating and staying present.* *If any of them emotionally left the discussion, ask them where they went. Remember, dissociation is a defense mechanism that you may have to cope with continually in the process of doing the curriculum.* *One way to help the women be present is to have them concentrate on the age that they are now, focus on the chair they are sitting in, and notice their feet on the ground. Also, have them breathe and be conscious of their breath for a moment. This is one way to help women ground themselves.*	One thing I hope you will take away from this group is that you are not alone in your experience with trauma. Here are some statistics to give us an idea of how often trauma occurs in women's lives. It is important to look at how common abuse is for women and girls because we often feel isolated, alone, or at fault for the abuse. For instance: **Violence against Women and Children** • One out of every four girls will be sexually abused before the age of fourteen (Hopper 1998). • More than two million cases of child abuse and neglect are reported each year in the United States. An estimated 150,000 to 200,000 new cases of sexual abuse occur each year (American Medical Association 1998). • Approximately 52 percent of child abuse and neglect victims are girls; 48 percent are boys (National Center on Child Abuse and Neglect 1998). • In 90 percent of child sexual abuse cases, victims are abused by someone they know or are related to, not a stranger (Tower 1993). • One study found that females are more than six times as likely as males to be victims of sexual assault. More specifically, 86 percent of all victims of sexual assault are female. The relative proportion of female victims increases with age. Sixty-nine percent of victims under age six are female; 73 percent under age twelve are female; these numbers reach 90 percent

TIME & TOPIC	FACILITATOR NOTES	DISCUSSION WITH WOMEN
		by age thirteen and 95 percent by age nineteen (Bureau of Justice Statistics [BJS] 2000b).

DISCUSSION WITH WOMEN (continued)

- The National Crime Victimization Survey found that, in 1996, more than two-thirds of the rapes and sexual assaults committed in the United States remained unreported (Ringel 1997).

- Every year in the United States, more than 5,000 women are murdered. Every day, four women are killed by their male partners (BJS 1998).

- Approximately 1.5 million women are raped or physically assaulted by an intimate partner each year in the United States. Because many victims are victimized more than once, approximately 4.8 million intimate partner rapes and physical assaults against women are committed annually (BJS 2000a).

- While relationship violence happens to women of every race and ethnic background, African American women are physically assaulted at a rate that is 35 percent higher than Caucasian women, and about two and a half times the rate of women of other races (National Coalition Against Domestic Violence 2000).

- During one calendar year, an assault against a female by her male partner occurred in thirty-five out of every one hundred couples (American Psychological Association 1996).

Family Violence

- Intimate partner violence made up 20 percent of all nonfatal violent crime experienced by women in 2001 (BJS 2003).

TIME & TOPIC	FACILITATOR NOTES	DISCUSSION WITH WOMEN
		• The negative effects on a child who witnesses violence against his or her mother (secondary victimization) appear to be low self-esteem, behavioral problems, reduced social competence, depression, and anxiety (Carlson 1990).
		• Women suffer injuries related to domestic violence about thirteen times more frequently than do men (American Psychological Association 1996).
		• There are four million cases of domestic violence in the United States each year. A woman is beaten every fifteen seconds (BJS 1998).
		• Both men and women who reported having been hit by their parents in childhood were found to be more likely to hit their own children (Cappell and Heiner 1990).
		Women in the Criminal Justice System
		• Women offenders have been victims of abuse six to ten times more often than women in the general population (Pollock 2002).
		• Between 23 and 37 percent of female offenders reported that they had been physically or sexually abused before the age of eighteen (BJS 1999).
		• In one prison study (California), 80 percent of the women offenders had experienced abuse—most often committed by family members or other intimates (Owen and Bloom 1995).
		• One-third of women in state prisons and one-fourth of women in jails said they had been raped (BJS 1999).
		• Two-thirds of women in criminal justice settings had been injured in a fight or assault (BJS 1999).

TIME & TOPIC	FACILITATOR NOTES	DISCUSSION WITH WOMEN
		• Women can be traumatized (or retraumatized if they have already experienced trauma in their lives) by the standard operating practices in criminal justice settings (denial of privacy, body searches, restraints, isolation) (Bloom, Owen, and Covington 2003). One woman who was incarcerated wrote: "I was very shocked when the police confided in my attorney that they believed I was an abused woman. Who, me abused? My husband had a quick temper and some personality quirks, and, yes, he had dropped me on the floor, knocked me out cold, and pushed me down the stairs; but, gee, I never had to go to the hospital. Little did I know that I would discover what constitutes abuse and how this affected me and my children." It may sound amazing that a woman might not know that she was abused, but it's not uncommon. Women often feel ashamed about the abuse they have suffered. They may think that the abuse is their fault. It may hurt so much to think about the abuse in their past that women in recovery may consider using addictive substances to deal with the pain. So it's important to know that abuse is never the victim's fault. Even if a child disobeys, the parent is never justified in doing things that harm the child. Even if a woman is drunk or flirtatious, a man is never justified in hitting her or forcing her to have sex.
	Remember to periodically check in with group members about how they are doing. You may need to help them ground themselves.	

Duplicating this page is illegal. Do not copy this material without written permission from the publisher.

73

TIME & TOPIC	FACILITATOR NOTES	DISCUSSION WITH WOMEN
Substance abuse and trauma		We have seen how common abuse is in women's lives. And for many women, trauma and substance abuse become linked. For some women, alcohol, drugs, or addictive behaviors such as overeating, gambling, and overworking help to ease the pain of abuse. Women who abuse substances have higher rates of childhood physical and sexual abuse than men and non-substance-abusing women (Covington and Surrey 1997). Also, women who abuse alcohol and other drugs are more vulnerable to being abused.
Gender differences with violence and abuse		Girls and boys are both at risk of physical, sexual, and emotional abuse when they are young. But the victimization rate changes as girls and boys grow older. In adolescence, for instance, girls are more likely than boys to continue to be abused, often by someone close to them such as a date or relative. Boys are less likely to be abused, but if they are, it is less likely to happen in an intimate relationship than it is from peers or rivals, such as gangs. When males are assaulted or abused, it is more likely to be committed in public and by strangers. Females are assaulted or abused more often in private and by someone they know. This pattern carries on into adulthood. Women are at risk from people they know and men from strangers and/or in war. Women in the United States are nine times more likely to be a victim of crime in the home than out on the streets (Donziger 1996). Violence is pervasive in our society, and many have become numb to it. For women and girls, those people who say "I love you" can also be their abusers. This

TIME & TOPIC	FACILITATOR NOTES	DISCUSSION WITH WOMEN
		dynamic can be emotionally crazy-making for females. It breaks down a woman's sense of trust, safety, and security in the world because she may not know if she is safe even within her intimate circle. Males do not have the same experience of abuse throughout the course of their lives.
Different responses to trauma		The terms *trauma, abuse,* and *post-traumatic stress disorder (PTSD)* are often used interchangeably. Sometimes people use the word *trauma* to describe an event, sometimes to describe a response to an event. One way to clarify these terms is to think of trauma as an event and a response; and abuse as one type of traumatic event. PTSD is a common response to trauma and abuse. Earlier we discussed the many types of traumatic events. The diagnostic manual used by mental health professionals defines trauma as "involving direct personal experience of an event that involves actual or threatened death or serious injury, or other threat to one's physical integrity; or witnessing an event that involves death, injury, or a threat to the physical integrity of another person; or learning about unexpected or violent death, serious harm, or threat of death or injury experienced by a family member or other close associate. The person's response to the event must involve intense fear, helplessness, or horror (or in children, the response must involve disorganized or agitated behavior" (American Psychiatric Association 2000, 463). Women may have different responses to violence and abuse due to coping skills that may be effective for a specific event.

TIME & TOPIC	FACILITATOR NOTES	DISCUSSION WITH WOMEN
		Sometimes, however, trauma has occurred but may not be recognized immediately because the violent event may have been perceived by the individual as normal.
		The effects of traumatic victimization often result in post-traumatic stress disorder. The symptoms of PTSD can be grouped into three categories:
		1. Reexperiencing (includes disturbed sleep, intrusive memories, flashbacks, distressing dreams, nightmares, reliving the event, a view of the world as unsafe)
		2. Numbing and avoiding (mistrust of others, isolation and disconnection, emotional numbness, low self-esteem, neglect of health, dissociation, ability to remember events or feelings but not both, memory loss for certain events, loss of faith and hope)
		3. Hyperarousal (intense emotions, difficulty sleeping, panic and anxiousness, self-harm, risky behaviors, irritability, anger, difficulty concentrating) (American Psychiatric Association 2000)
		There are two types of PTSD: simple and complex. Simple PTSD is from a single incident (such as an earthquake or auto accident), usually as an adult. Complex PTSD is from repeated incidents (such as childhood sexual abuse or domestic violence). Generally, there are more symptoms and a more complicated recovery process with the complex PTSD (Herman 1997; Najavits 2002).
		In our sessions, we will explore together our responses to different situations, understand why we respond the way we do, and learn new ways to respond.

TIME & TOPIC	FACILITATOR NOTES	DISCUSSION WITH WOMEN
20 min. **Exercise:** *Creating Safety*		Safety is an important issue for every woman. If you have been abused or have experienced trauma, the need for safety can feel even more of a priority. Safety can be viewed on two levels: external safety and internal safety. External safety issues involve actions we take in our surroundings. We may lock our doors, choose not to go out alone at night, or unlist our telephone number. We do things to try to keep ourselves physically safe in our environment.
	Brainstorm ideas with the group about what they would do to reduce agitation and stress and to calm themselves. Make a list on the easel pad.	Internal safety is how we take care of our emotions and feelings. If we feel overwhelmed, sad, angry, lonely, frightened, or stressed, we need to have ways to take care of ourselves. Sometimes we find internal safety actions harder to take. Yet, our internal safety is just as important as our external safety. We will be learning techniques in this group to help comfort and nurture ourselves and to help us pay attention to our internal safety.
		We can learn new self-soothing techniques from each other. You may find it helpful to have an object that you can keep with you and focus on when you need to comfort yourself. Let us do an exercise that will help you find your own self-soothing object.
	Give directions slowly. *Refer to visualization tips on page 52.* *Remember, some women may feel too anxious to close their eyes. Have them focus on an object with their eyes open.*	1. Close your eyes. Relax. . . . Take a few deep breaths. . . . Think of a place that makes you feel comfortable and secure. It might be a new place or someplace you have been to. It might be a favorite chair, or it might be your bed. . . . It might be a place you have created in your imagination—at the beach, in the water, in a garden or at a lake, in a beautiful meadow, in the snow, or at the top of a hill. If you cannot think of any place

TIME & TOPIC	FACILITATOR NOTES	DISCUSSION WITH WOMEN
		where you really feel good, think of a place where you felt free from fear, relaxed, or maybe even bored.
	Pause for one to two minutes to let the women totally experience the picture.	2. Keep your eyes closed and notice all the details in that picture. What do you see, hear, smell, feel, or taste? Experience every part.
		3. Now make any changes to the picture that would enhance the serenity and security of the experience. You can take things out or add things in. Nod your head when you have a picture in your mind.
		4. Enjoy this place and embrace the peacefulness of it. Keep your eyes closed. Now, let your mind choose a souvenir or symbol that will remind you of this experience in the future. The symbol can be an object, sight, sound, or sensation. Take a minute to receive your symbol. When you have it, take time to look at it, feel it, and stay connected with it.
		5. When you have your symbol, slowly open your eyes and begin to focus again on the here and now. When you are fully present, think back to the symbol.
	Give the group time to draw their self-soothing symbols in their workbooks.	If you turn to page 7 in your workbook, you'll find space to draw a picture of what you visualized.
	Discuss.	What feelings do you have when you think of the symbol (e.g., comfort, security, safety)?
	Ask the women to share their symbols with each other.	Even though we are all unique and probably had different pictures in our minds, sharing our images with the group can give each of us ideas of places and symbols of comfort.

TIME & TOPIC	FACILITATOR NOTES	DISCUSSION WITH WOMEN
	The following activity is optional. *It may be difficult for women in correctional settings to find and/or carry objects.*	For the next session, find an object that will remind you of the symbol you chose. Maybe it will be something that you can easily carry with you. Look at it when you want to bring back those safe, comforting feelings. If you cannot find an object, keep copies of your drawing in places where you can easily get to them, such as in your purse or pocket, on the refrigerator, in your locker, or on a mirror.
8 min. **Reflection and Homework**	*Discuss.*	How does it feel right now to have created a safe place for yourself? Your homework assignment, Creating Safety, on page 7 of your workbook, gives you an opportunity to practice ways to calm and soothe yourself. 1. Name some ways you have taken care of yourself when you have been afraid. 2. What are some other things you can imagine doing in the future? 3. Write about an experience where you calmed yourself, or write about the ways you have seen or heard other women take care of themselves. 4. Work on drawing your symbol or souvenir. You might want to make copies of it to keep in your pocket or purse, hang on a mirror, or keep in a locker.

Power and Abuse

■ Time

1 hour 30 minutes

■ Session Goal

Women will recognize the connection between power and abuse in our society.

■ Participant Learning Objectives

1. To understand how social messages impact women's lives

2. To think critically about gender roles and expectations

3. To understand the connection between power and abuse

■ Session Overview

- Gender Expectations
- *Exercise: Role Reversal*
- Making the Connection between Abuse and Power
- *Exercise: Grounding*
- The Power and Control Wheel
- *Reflection and Homework*

■ Materials and Equipment Needed

- Easel pad, felt pens, masking tape
- *Circle of Stones* (Duerk 1993) *(optional)*
- Participant's workbook
- Cassette or CD player and relaxing music
- Tissues
- VCR and monitor
- *Beyond Trauma* client video

Power and Abuse

TIME & TOPIC	FACILITATOR NOTES	DISCUSSION WITH WOMEN
2 min. **Quiet time**	*Allow a few minutes of silence before the session begins. You may want to play some soft music during this time. You will also find excellent excerpts to read from* Circle of Stones *(Duerk 1993).*	Let us be silent for a minute or two to give ourselves time to unwind, relax, and focus on where we are now.
15 min. **Check-in**	*The check-in time is a brief time for women to talk about how they are doing since the last group session or raise specific questions or issues that came up based on what was discussed last time. It is important that check-ins be kept brief. Any major individual issues will require an individual appointment time, set right after the session.* *Have them share their homework assignment.*	What have you been feeling and thinking about coming to the second session of the group? Share an experience where you calmed or soothed yourself or how you have seen other women take care of themselves.
Goal for the session		In this session we will be focusing on the connection between power and abuse in our society.

TIME & TOPIC	FACILITATOR NOTES	DISCUSSION WITH WOMEN
15 min. **Gender expectations**		Today we will begin by looking at some of the differences between women and men. We will be focusing on gender differences. Gender is the experience of being raised as female or male.
	List the questions and answers on the easel pad.	Let's start by discussing these questions: • How are boys and girls treated differently as children? • What are the social messages boys get? • How are boys supposed to be? • What are the social messages girls get? • How are girls supposed to be? Gender expectations are a set of social expectations, defined by society, religion, culture, family, peers, and others, and based on whether we are male or female. (Sexual differences are biologically determined.)
	Discuss.	How do we learn these gender expectations and roles?
	Discuss and write ideas on the easel pad. They may include be quiet, be polite, be nurturing, be a caregiver, don't talk back, don't be too smart, be dependent, put your own needs aside, be sexy, be a good housekeeper, be pretty, be dependent, always be available for men, etc.	What does it mean to "act like a woman"?
	Discuss and write ideas on the easel pad. They may include be aggressive, be the breadwinner, be emotionally unavailable, be mean, be tough, don't cry, be successful, be strong, be in control, be dominant over women.	What does it mean to "act like a man"?

TIME & TOPIC	FACILITATOR NOTES	DISCUSSION WITH WOMEN
		Just by the fact that we are female, there are defined ways of acting or being (taking on a particular role) in our culture. Gender expectations begin when we are infants and influence the way we act and the choices we make throughout our lives. What would it be like if our roles were changed?
30 min. **Exercise:** *Role Reversal* **Video:** *Beyond Trauma* Client video • READING "FANTASY" • DEBRIEFING	*Read the fantasy slowly, so that the fantasy aspect is reinforced and so that there is time for the images it conjures up to be realized by the listeners.* *This fantasy is also on the video. You have the option of doing the role-reversal exercise yourself or using the video.* *Show video: Segment 2*	I am going to read a role-reversal guided imagery. This is a "fantasy." Close your eyes as I read this scenario, and put yourself into the fantasy. **Woman—Which Includes Man, of Course** There is much concern today about the future of man, which means, of course, both men and women—generic Man. For a woman to take exception to this use of the term "man" is often seen as defensive hair-splitting by an "emotional female." The following experience is an invitation to awareness in which you are asked to feel into, and stay with, your feelings through each step, letting them absorb you. If you start thinking too much, try to turn it down and let your feelings again surface to your awareness. Consider reversing the generic term "Man." Think of the future of "Woman" which, of course, includes both women and men. Feel into that, sense the meaning to you—as a woman—as a man. Think of it always being that way, every day of your life. Feel the ever-presence of woman and feel the non-presence of man. Absorb

TIME & TOPIC	FACILITATOR NOTES	DISCUSSION WITH WOMEN
		what it tells you about the importance and value of being woman—or being man.
		Recall that everything you have ever read, all your life, uses only female pronouns—she, her—meaning both boys and girls, both women and men. Recall that most of the voices on the radio and most of the faces on TV are women's—when important events are covered, on commercials, and on the late night talk shows.
		Feel into the fact that women are the leaders, the power centers, the prime movers. Man, whose natural role is husband and father, fulfills himself through nurturing children and making the home a refuge for woman. This is only natural to balance the biological role of woman, who devotes her entire body to the race through pregnancy.
		Then feel further into the obvious biological explanation for woman as the ideal—her genital construction. By design, female genitals are compact and internal, protected by her body. Male genitals are so exposed that he must be protected from outside attack to ensure the perpetuation of the race. His vulnerability clearly requires sheltering.
		Thus, by nature, males are more passive than females, and have a desire in sexual relations to be symbolically engulfed by the protective body of the woman. Males psychologically yearn for this protection, fully realizing their masculinity at this time—feeling exposed and vulnerable at other times. The male is not fully adult until he has overcome his infantile tendency to penis orgasm and has achieved the mature surrender of the testicle orgasm. He then feels himself a "whole man" when engulfed by the women.

TIME & TOPIC	FACILITATOR NOTES	DISCUSSION WITH WOMEN
		If the male denies these feelings, he is unconsciously rejecting his masculinity. Therapy is thus indicated to help him adjust to his own nature. Of course, therapy is administered by a woman who has the education and wisdom to facilitate openness leading to the male's growth and self-actualization. To help him feel into his defensive emotionality, he is invited to get in touch with the "child" in him. He remembers his sister's jeering at his primitive genitals that "flop around foolishly." She can run, climb, and ride horseback unencumbered. Obviously, since she is free to move, she is encouraged to develop her body and mind to prepare for her active responsibilities of adult womanhood. The male vulnerability needs female protection, so he is taught the less active, caring virtues of homemaking. Because of his clitoris-envy, he learns to strap up his genitals, and learns to feel ashamed and unclean because of his nocturnal emissions. Instead, he is encouraged to keep his body lean and dream of getting married, waiting for the time of his fulfillment—when "his woman" gives him a girl-child to carry on the family name. He knows that if it is a boy-child he has failed somehow, but they can try again. In getting to your feelings on being a woman—on being a man—stay with the sensing you are now experiencing. As the words begin to surface, say what you feel from inside you. Now, come out of the fantasy slowly, gradually opening your eyes and holding on to your feelings.
	(Reprinted by permission of Theodora Wells from "Woman—Which Includes Man, of Course: An Experience in Awareness," copyright © 1970, 1972.)	

TIME & TOPIC	FACILITATOR NOTES	DISCUSSION WITH WOMEN
Debrief role-reversal exercise	*On the easel pad, draw a line down the middle of the paper. Write "woman" on the top of one column and "man" at the top of the other column.*	
	As you ask the discussion questions, write the women's responses on the pad.	Let's talk about the role reversal exercise.
	Women typically respond with answers such as in charge, strong, powerful, respected, not vulnerable, responsible, important, safe. Some women will say that this scenario is wonderful for women and everything is awful for men, while other women will feel that there are good and bad aspects of both sexes in this kind of system.	1. How do you think a woman in this fantasy might feel or react?
	Answers often include disempowered, angry, vulnerable, scared, emasculated, not valued, and unimportant.	2. How do you think a man in this fantasy might feel or react?
	Most women see that men would have the greater risk of depression in this fantasy.	3. Who do you think is at greater risk for depression in this fantasy?
	Most women recognize the man is more likely to have low self-esteem.	4. Who do you think will have low self-esteem?
	You may need to explain that "codependent" means having one's life revolve around another person's addiction. Most see the man as falling into this role in the fantasy.	5. Who is more likely to be considered "codependent"?

TIME & TOPIC	FACILITATOR NOTES	DISCUSSION WITH WOMEN
	Most women say the man.	6. Who is more likely to feel guilt and shame?
	Most women say the man.	7. Who is more likely to feel negative about her or his body?
	Most women say that the men are at the greatest risk for abuse. This is a key point: When men in our society have the most power, then women are at greatest risk for abuse. When we reverse the roles and women have more power than men, men are at risk. This discussion will emphasize the relationship between power and abuse.	8. Who is more likely to be abused? For those with less power, the risk for abuse is greatest. Reading this fantasy helps us see how our social structure is based on a dominant and subordinate model. For instance, if you are a person in a less powerful group, you probably know quite a bit about the dominant culture. But the dominant group tends not to know as much about what it is like to be in a subordinate role. One example is that women tend to know a lot more about men than men know about women. Blacks know a lot more about whites than whites know about blacks. Lesbians and gay men know more about straight people than straight people know about lesbians and gay men. Subordinates learn as much as possible about the dominant culture in order to survive in that world. Dominants do not need to know about subordinates to survive and, in fact, may feel that they have nothing to learn from subordinates. There is also a myth in a dominant/subordinate culture that says dominants will protect subordinates. Men are supposed to protect women, and adults are supposed to protect children. However, in reality, dominant people frequently abuse and devalue subordinates. Think about your experience as a woman, a child, a person of color, an employee, or another subordinate role.

TIME & TOPIC	FACILITATOR NOTES	DISCUSSION WITH WOMEN
		Now think about what it is like to be the adult, the white person, or the rich person who can take advantage of someone with less power.
	You may find that some women do not like the fantasy because it sets up a world that still uses power over others. You can respond by saying that you agree: An imbalanced system in which some people are dominant and some are subordinate is not good for anyone.	This fantasy can help us see and feel what it is like to have power and control. Powerlessness is a huge issue for women and one we will explore together in the coming sessions.
Making the connection between abuse and power	*See page 84 and list on easel pad.* *Discuss.* *Elicit responses from the group and write them on the easel pad. Examples might include the list on the right.*	Let's revisit the messages that women are often given. How do these messages help or harm a woman's sense of power and her sense of self in the world? Let's see how power and roles relate to abuse, violence, and trauma. • Abuser uses power over victim. • Abuse takes power away from the victim. • Victim feels powerless against abuser and in many aspects of her life. • Victim feels trapped or locked in a role. • Victim feels isolated, so there is no strength or power from others who could help. Many women who experience or witness violence, particularly actions that threaten their life and safety, are traumatized by events that "overwhelm the ordinary system of care that give people a sense of control,

TIME & TOPIC	FACILITATOR NOTES	DISCUSSION WITH WOMEN
		connection, and meaning" (Herman 1997). In other words, a woman's sense of self, self-worth, and self-power are diminished by the abuse.
5 min. **Exercise:** *Grounding*	*You may find that some of the women are uncomfortable, distracted, or having negative feelings in response to the exercises. Grounding techniques are ways to help the women detach or disconnect from inner emotional discomfort by focusing on the outer world. Grounding is one way to help the women become empowered.*	You may find yourself feeling uncomfortable and distracted at times or having negative feelings. Grounding techniques are ways to detach or disconnect from inner emotional discomfort by focusing on the outer world. Grounding is one way to become empowered. With your eyes open, remind yourself of your name, your age, where you are now, the day of the week, the date, and the city. Then notice the environment you are in—the size of the room, color of the walls, furniture in the room, pictures on the wall, height of the ceiling, and so on. This is an exercise you can use in or out of group.
15 min. **The Power and Control Wheel**	*Make a list on the easel pad of the various forms of abuse:* • *emotional abuse* • *physical abuse* • *economic abuse* • *sexual abuse* • *coercion and threats* • *intimidation* • *isolation* • *using children* • *using male privilege* • *minimizing* • *denying* • *blaming*	**Power and Control Wheel** (Duluth Domestic Abuse Intervention Project, 202 East Superior St., Duluth, MN 55802) The Power and Control Wheel is in your workbook on page 12.

Duplicating this page is illegal. Do not copy this material without written permission from the publisher.

91

TIME & TOPIC	FACILITATOR NOTES	DISCUSSION WITH WOMEN
		It was developed in the domestic violence field, and it shows that power and control are at the center of violence. We will be using this for our homework.
	Have the women spend a few minutes in pairs to develop examples of how each form of abuse might look. Then have them come back into the circle and begin to share their examples with the rest of the group.	You will see that the Power and Control Wheel is divided into parts, or segments. Each of these represents ways someone can be abusive to another.
8 min. **Reflection and Homework**	*Discuss.*	What is one thing you learned today that surprised you? In this session we discussed power and abuse. Those without power are at greatest risk for abuse. Those with power may use their privilege to abuse others. For your homework, work on filling in examples for the Power and Control Wheel on page 13 in your workbook. You may work in pairs if you would like to. Try to give any additional examples that you can think of.

Session Notes

MODULE B

The Impact of Trauma
on Women's Lives

Session 3

Reactions to Trauma

PAGE 95

Session 4

How Trauma Impacts Our Lives

PAGE 109

MODULE B: SESSION 3

Reactions to Trauma

▧ Time

1 hour 30 minutes

▧ Session Goal

Women will recognize and understand the reactions to trauma.

▧ Participant Learning Objectives

1. To identify the different types of interpersonal violence (emotional, physical, sexual abuse)
2. To understand the biological nature of traumatic reactions
3. To recognize the symptoms associated with trauma

▧ Session Overview

- Types of Abuse
- Biological Reactions to Trauma
- Symptoms Associated with Trauma
- Symptoms Following Trauma
- Symptoms That Typically Take Longer to Develop
- Trauma and the Brain
- Fight or Flight Response
- *Exercise: Reconnection with the Body*
- *Reflection and Homework*

▧ Materials and Equipment Needed

- Easel pad, felt pens, masking tape
- Small bags with various items
- Cassette or CD player and relaxing music
- Tissues
- VCR and monitor
- Participant's workbook
- *Beyond Trauma* client video

Reactions to Trauma

TIME & TOPIC°	FACILITATOR NOTES	DISCUSSION WITH WOMEN
2 min. **Quiet time**	*You may want to play soft music.*	Let us just sit quietly for a few minutes to let ourselves unwind, relax, and turn our attention to where we are now.
10 min. **Check-in**	*A question you may want to use for check-ins is, "What did you take from the last session and how have you applied it in your life?"* *Discuss and have women share two examples for each segment of the Power and Control Wheel. Refer to the labeled wheel at the side for additional examples.* (Duluth Domestic Abuse Intervention Project, 202 East Superior St., Duluth, MN 55802)	How is everyone doing today? In the last session we talked about power and control and its connection to abuse. In your workbook you filled in sections of the Power and Control Wheel. **Power and Control Wheel** PHYSICAL VIOLENCE SEXUAL **USING COERCION AND THREATS** Making and/or carrying out threats to do something to hurt her • threatening to leave her, to commit suicide to report her to welfare • making her drop charges • making her do illegal things **USING INTIMIDATION** Making her afraid by using looks, actions, gestures • smashing things • destroying her property • abusing pets • displaying weapons **USING ECONOMIC ABUSE** Preventing her from getting or keeping a job • making her ask for money • giving her an allowance • taking her money • not letting her know about or have access to family income **USING EMOTIONAL ABUSE** Putting her down • making her feel bad about herself • making her think she's crazy • playing mind games • humiliating her • making her feel guilty **POWER AND CONTROL** **USING MALE PRIVILEGE** Treating her like a servant • making all the big decisions • acting like the "master of the castle" • being the one to define men's and women's roles **USING ISOLATION** Controlling what she does, who she sees and talks to, what she reads, where she goes • limiting her outside involvement • using jealousy to justify actions **USING CHILDREN** Making her feel guilty about the children • using the children to relay messages • threatening to take the children **MINIMIZING DENYING AND BLAMING** Making light of the abuse and not taking her concerns about it seriously • saying the abuse didn't happen • shifting responsibility for abusive behavior • saying she caused it PHYSICAL VIOLENCE SEXUAL

TIME & TOPIC	FACILITATOR NOTES	DISCUSSION WITH WOMEN
Goal for the session		Today we will be learning about reactions to trauma.
30 min. **Types of abuse**		We have been looking at the Power and Control Wheel, and each of you has given examples of various forms of abuse. Let us look more specifically at physical, sexual, and emotional abuse. As we know, these are forms of interpersonal violence that are common in women's lives. *Emotional abuse* includes playing mind games, name-calling, constant criticizing, withholding approval or affection as punishment, humiliating someone publicly or privately, abusing pets, threatening, manipulating, and blaming. *Physical abuse* includes pushing, slapping, kicking, choking, locking someone out of the house, threatening someone with a weapon, harassing someone to the point of physical illness, restraining (holding someone down, pinning the person's arms), depriving someone of sleep, biting, shaking, spitting, and deliberately giving someone a sexually transmitted disease. *Sexual abuse* includes rape, coercion, unwanted or inappropriate touch, sex after a beating or an illness, sexual criticism, forcing sex in front of others, treating others as sex objects, and nonconsensual sadistic sexual acts.
Biological reactions to trauma		Now let us continue to look at what can happen if a woman is traumatized by abuse. Traumatic reactions that are experienced both in the inner self (thoughts and feelings) and the outer self (relationships and behaviors) are a normal response to an abnormal or extreme situation.

TIME & TOPIC	FACILITATOR NOTES	DISCUSSION WITH WOMEN
		People respond to danger and threats in a variety of ways: instinctively (or automatically), physically, and psychologically (emotionally, cognitively). For example, if we are overwhelmed by a threat and are unable to fight or flee, we may instinctively go into a "freezing response" and become immobilized. Or perhaps our nervous system is highly aroused and our consciousness seems to leave our body. This is known as "dissociation." Grounding techniques are useful tools for dealing with dissociation.
Symptoms associated with trauma		Let us talk more specifically about some of the symptoms associated with trauma. • *Hyperarousal* is one of the most common reaction to trauma. It includes difficulty breathing (panting; shallow, rapid breaths), increased heart rate, cold sweats, muscular tension, tingling, racing thoughts, and worry. • *Constriction* alters breathing, muscle tone, and posture. It constricts blood vessels in the skin, arms, legs, and internal organs, and tenses muscles. Hyperarousal and constriction describe some of the physical responses. • *Dissociation* occurs when your mind disconnects from the event or physical reality of what is happening. This is a mind-body split. Often women describe this as "losing time." This can also include loss of memory. • *Denial* is like dissociation, only not as severe. A woman ignores or fails to acknowledge a feeling or situation, or acts as though it is unimportant. Dissociation and denial are psychological responses that act as coping mechanisms.

TIME & TOPIC	FACILITATOR NOTES	DISCUSSION WITH WOMEN
		Sometimes it looks like women are denying abuse (remember, abuse is one form of trauma) when actually they are not sure they have been abused. Here are five questions to answer about events and experiences in your relationships that may concern you: 1. Was there full consent? Was there coercion? 2. Was there an element of betrayal, loss of trust? 3. Was there violence, pain, restriction, force, or bodily harm? 4. Did it feel like abuse to you? 5. Did you feel afraid? *Feelings of helplessness, immobility, or freezing* may also occur. Peter Levine, a well-known expert in the field of trauma, says that if hyperarousal is the nervous system's accelerator, immobility is its brake. When both occur at the same time, a feeling of overwhelming helplessness and power-lessness results. This is not a perception. The body feels truly paralyzed (Levine 1997). Remember, these are normal responses to abnormal or extreme situations. This is what happens when the body is overwhelmed.
Symptoms following trauma		Some symptoms show up immediately following a traumatic event. Some show up later. Examples of typical symptoms include • sleep disturbance, nightmares • exaggerated emotional and startled reactions to noises, quick movements, etc. • hyperactivity, restlessness • hypervigilance

TIME & TOPIC	FACILITATOR NOTES	DISCUSSION WITH WOMEN
		• abrupt mood swings • fear of going crazy • flashbacks • sensitivity to sound, light, smell, taste, touch • fear of losing control • a desire for alcohol or other drugs In an earlier session, we mentioned post-traumatic stress disorder, or PTSD. It is a name for a cluster of symptoms. It is a diagnosis often given to survivors of trauma who begin to experience many of the above symptoms a month or more after the event. When this happens, the feelings a woman experiences are very real and vivid, as if the event were actually happening all over again.
Symptoms that typically take longer to develop		These are symptoms that typically take longer to develop: • panic attacks, anxiety, phobias • mental blankness or being "spacey" • avoidance behavior • attraction to dangerous situations • frequent anger or crying • exaggerated or diminished sexual activity • amnesia and forgetfulness • inability to love, nurture, or bond with other individuals • fear of dying or having a shortened life • self-harming behavior • cravings (particularly if chemically dependent)

TIME & TOPIC	FACILITATOR NOTES	DISCUSSION WITH WOMEN
		These symptoms may take even longer to develop and may be preceded by the above symptoms: • fatigue or low energy • physical health problems, such as a depleted immune system, thyroid dysfunction, psychosomatic illnesses such as neck and back problems, asthma, digestive distress, spastic colon, severe premenstrual syndrome • eating disorders • diminished emotional responses • inability to make commitments • depression • feelings of isolation, detachment • reduced ability to make decisions, formulate plans, and carry them out It is important to listen to our bodies and understand how one or more, or a cluster, of these symptoms may be a reason to seek help and to understand the impact trauma has had on our lives.
Trauma and the brain **Video:** *Beyond Trauma* ————— Client video • TRAUMA AND BRAIN • GROUP COMMENTS	*Show video: Segment 3.*	Trauma also impacts how the brain functions. People under stress often process and organize information differently. For example, research on the brain has shown that child abuse, one form of trauma, can cause serious damage to the structure and functioning of the developing brain itself. Extreme stress can change the brain to cause a person to exhibit various anti-social, though adaptive, behaviors. Physical, emotional, or sexual abuse or any other major stress can set off a series of physical changes that alter a child's brain in order for it to cope with a dangerous world.

TIME & TOPIC	FACILITATOR NOTES	DISCUSSION WITH WOMEN
		When trauma impacts the brain, it can result in emotional changes. Problems such as dissociation, flashbacks, and confusion (racing or jumbled thoughts), which we discussed earlier, may all stem from the impact of trauma on the brain. Fear from a traumatic event is experienced in the mind. Some people experience and reexperience these thoughts even though they do not want to have them and try not to have them.
		Many women talk about frightening thoughts "invading" their minds—sometimes at uncontrollable times (after something triggers their memory of the traumatic event) and in their dreams. Nightmares are not uncommon. Sometimes a woman may have "night terrors," where she wakes up screaming and sweating yet cannot recall what she was dreaming about. This can make the woman feel that, even when she is in her bed, at home, during the night, she still is not safe. Sometimes these invasions in her mind make her feel like she is going crazy or losing control of her mind.
	Discuss.	Have any of you experienced this kind of thing?
	Discuss. A typical response might be for others to tell them to "just put it all behind you" or "move on."	If you have let others know that a traumatic event has impacted your life, what has been their reaction?
		Trauma can also cause problems like depression, anxiety, rage, and feelings of chronic emptiness. There is also a connection with addiction. Understanding that trauma can change brain chemistry (just like substance abuse can change brain chemistry) can help you see the connection between trauma and what is going on physically and emotionally.

TIME & TOPIC	FACILITATOR NOTES	DISCUSSION WITH WOMEN
Fight or flight response		Women react to trauma on several different levels, including physical, mental, and behavioral. Our physical reactions are automatic and done without our control. For example, when faced with danger, our bodies automatically respond. Most people, and other animals, respond to stress or a trauma with a "fight or flight" response. The brain sends a signal to the body to be on alert—an increase in heart rate, an increase in blood pressure and muscle tension, dilation of the eyes, shallow breathing, flushed skin, tunnel vision, and a flow of adrenaline, the release of certain chemicals from the brain into the body. For those who have had a traumatic experience, the fight or flight mechanism can chronically begin to function poorly, or not at all. For example, a woman may be overly sensitive to a mildly stressful event, or she may shut down and become "numb" (psychically and/or physically). All people who survive a traumatic event experience the reaction to fear and anxiety physically. The body has stored this reaction and, when triggered, returns to what it knows about the past trauma; thus, it can reexperience the same level of fear or danger. The body reacts as though it is reliving the traumatic events of the past. As we learn about the signs and symptoms associated with trauma, we can more fully understand the struggles that impact women's lives: addiction, self-harming behavior, a heightened startle response, physical pain, muscle tension, and eating disorders.

TIME & TOPIC	FACILITATOR NOTES	DISCUSSION WITH WOMEN
35 min. **Exercise:** *Reconnection with the Body*		In this module, we have learned that dissociation and disconnection from the body are some ways that women are impacted by trauma. The next two exercises will allow you to explore the complexities and subtleties of your connection to your own body. Here we'll learn ways to begin the reconnection—to help you read and know your own body.
	Remember, some women may need to keep their eyes open.	First, please close your eyes. . . . Then slowly touch your face, arm, or hand. . . . See if you can focus mentally on its temperature. . . . Is it warm or cold? . . . Then focus on the pressure of your touch. . . . Is it light or firm? . . . Then focus on the texture . . . smooth or rough? . . . Finally, focus on the presence or absence of moisture. . . . Is it absolutely dry, or is there some moisture? Just try to relax into the sensations that you are feeling. Open your eyes.
	Discuss.	• What was your experience of connecting with your body? • Was it difficult? • Was it easy? • What feelings did you have as you did this exercise?
	You can also have the women use this exercise (eyes open) as a grounding exercise.	Periodically try to practice this exercise so that it becomes easier for you to focus on these four basic sensations: • temperature • pressure • texture • moisture

TIME & TOPIC	FACILITATOR NOTES	DISCUSSION WITH WOMEN
Texture and Sensation	*Have the women close their eyes. (For women who keep eyes open, ask them to look away from the bag.) Give each woman a small zip-closure bag with a variety of objects in it. You can have enough bags with objects for each woman to get a bag. Or you can have several bags that get passed around. The bags might contain velvet, satin, fur, feathers, plastic, stone, metal, sandpaper, etc. They should be items that feel different from one another. (Or the bags can contain items with strong, distinct odors, e.g., lemon peel, garlic clove, rose petal.)*	Both abuse and addiction can numb our bodies and impact our sensuality. This exercise is about learning to feel different sensations.
	With her eyes closed, have each woman open her bag and feel the objects inside. (If sharing bags, after a minute or so, have the women pass their bags and objects to the woman next to them.) The idea is to be able to feel a variety of physical sensations or smells.	Close your eyes or look away from the bag that is given to you. Spend a few minutes feeling each item in the bag (or smelling each item).
	Discuss the exercise. Have the women describe what they felt.	What happened for you in this exercise? Could you sense all the different shapes and textures?

TIME & TOPIC	FACILITATOR NOTES	DISCUSSION WITH WOMEN
13 min. **Reflection and Homework**		What was the most meaningful (important) part of today's group? We mentioned earlier that trauma is very common in women's lives, and many women have experienced multiple traumatic events. In your homework exercise on page 20 of your workbook, you will have an opportunity to look back at your history of trauma at different points in your life. (You may want to practice your grounding exercise when you do your history chart.) Remember, trauma can be many things, including physical, emotional, and sexual abuse. If you are questioning whether an event was abusive, here are the five important questions to ask yourself that we discussed earlier: 1. Was there full consent? Was there coercion? 2. Was there an element of betrayal, loss of trust? 3. Was there violence, pain, restriction, force, or bodily harm? 4. Did it feel like abuse to you? 5. Did you feel afraid? Charting the trauma and abuse you have faced in your life allows you to see the strength, resiliency, and survival skills that have brought you to where you are today. Pick three traumatic experiences: one from childhood, one from adolescence, and one from adulthood, if possible. If not, just pick any three from any time period.

Duplicating this page is illegal. Do not copy this material without written permission from the publisher.

107

TIME & TOPIC	FACILITATOR NOTES	DISCUSSION WITH WOMEN

	CHILD	ADOLESCENT	ADULT
A. Event			
B. Life before the event			
C. Life after the event			
D. Overall impact of the traumatic events			

In the boxes, list

A. the event

B. how life was before the event

C. how life was after the event

D. how you view the overall impact of these traumas in your life (Did the events impact your life? If so, how?)

You can use the five questions (on page 107) to determine whether these events were examples of abuse in your own life.

Let us take a moment to reflect on what we have covered here. It is important to remember that any memories you visit are in the past. Any feelings you have are part of the process of healing, and right now you are safe.

Session Notes

MODULE B: SESSION 4

How Trauma Impacts Our Lives

■ Time

1 hour 30 minutes

■ Session Goal

Women will understand the impact of trauma in their lives.

■ Participant Learning Objectives

1. To learn how traumatic events affect women's lives
2. To understand what a trigger is
3. To creatively express through collage how trauma has impacted a woman's life

■ Session Overview

- Trauma and Its Aftermath
- *Exercise: The Impact of Violence, Abuse, and Trauma in Your Life (Collage)*
- *Reflection and Homework*

■ Materials and Equipment Needed

- Easel pad, felt pens, masking tape
- Participant's workbook
- Cassette or CD player and relaxing music
- Magazines for collage exercise
- A piece of poster board for each participant
- Glue sticks and scissors for group to share
- Tissues

Duplicating this page is illegal. Do not copy this material without written permission from the publisher.

109

How Trauma Impacts Our Lives

TIME & TOPIC	FACILITATOR NOTES	DISCUSSION WITH WOMEN
2 min. **Quiet time**	*You may want to play soft music.*	Let us just sit quietly for a few minutes to let ourselves unwind, relax, and turn our attention to where we are now.
10 min. **Check-in**		The last question on your homework assignment was about how trauma has impacted your life. Does anyone want to share?
Goal for the session		Today we are going to continue to look at the impact of trauma in our lives.
20 min. **Trauma and its aftermath**		After a traumatic event, many women say they feel they are "losing control" of their lives. These feelings of loss of control come from the event, and they can affect many parts of a woman's life. Many women reexperience the traumatic incident in their memories, thoughts, and dreams. These reexperienced traumas can be so intense that it feels as though the event is happening all over again. When this is happening, some women find it hard to concentrate and keep their minds on a task or action they are doing—even something as simple as watching TV. This can often add to feeling out of control. A woman's self-image may change after a traumatic incident. She may find that she neglects herself and feels worthless. She may feel labeled or tarnished in some way.

TIME & TOPIC	FACILITATOR NOTES	DISCUSSION WITH WOMEN
		This may be particularly true if there was public knowledge of the event and little support for her. Some women experience depression, a sense of isolation, and sadness. A woman may find that she cries often for no apparent reason, that she feels she cannot or should not have fun anymore, that she has lost interest in many things, and that she has no energy. Getting out of bed in the morning may feel like it is becoming a chore. It is not unusual for a woman's relationships to be disrupted, either. She may find, along with the depression, that she withdraws from others. Support from friends or family is particularly important during this time. Her sexuality may also be impacted by the trauma. This may be true whether or not the trauma involved sexual abuse. Some women state they lose interest in sex, while others engage in more sex than usual. Fear and anxiety may become a part of each day for women. This is perhaps the most common reaction of women who have experienced trauma. If the cause of the trauma is still present, nearby, or at large, a woman may feel she is still in danger. She may feel jittery, overcautious, or unable to function in certain situations (she may be afraid to leave her home, be alone, go to locations near where the event took place, be in situations that remind her of the event, or see people who have anything to do with the event, whether they were positively or negatively involved). Women's lives often become limited and constricted due to fear of harm.

TIME & TOPIC	FACILITATOR NOTES	DISCUSSION WITH WOMEN
	Ask if any of this sounds familiar? Have they, a friend, or a family member had this experience? Discuss.	As mentioned earlier, trauma can impact a woman's relationships. Some of the relationship problems might include • idealizing or overvaluing relationships • fear of commitment • self-imposed isolation • triangulating with others • humiliating interactions • involvement in abusive or criticizing relationships • difficulty trusting self or others with intimacy • tolerating patterns of abuse or excessive neediness • emotional and physical caretaking of others at expense of self
	Again, ask if any of this relates to their experience? Or, maybe a friend or family member has had these difficulties.	Traumatic events, particularly sexual abuse, can impact a woman's sexual relationships. The impact of abuse might include • avoidance of or fear of sex • approaching sex as obligation • negative feelings with touch • difficulty with arousal, sensation • vaginal pain • emotional distance during sex (spacing out) • disturbing sexual thoughts and images • compulsive or inappropriate sexual behavior • difficulty in intimate relationships During the abusive incident, a woman may have feared physical harm or death. Sights, smells, and sounds associated with the event may be prevalent and very real to her for

TIME & TOPIC	FACILITATOR NOTES	DISCUSSION WITH WOMEN
		weeks, months, or even years later. They may act as "triggers"—putting her back into the traumatic experience.

A *trigger* is an external stimulus that sets off a physical or emotional reaction in a person. The stimulus can be a sound, another person, a place, a smell, a behavior—almost anything that consciously or subconsciously reminds the woman of the past trauma.

Women react to trauma on several different levels. Physical reactions are automatic and happen without our control. For example, when faced with danger, our bodies automatically respond with a fight or flight response. If a woman who has been traumatized is later triggered by a stimulus, her body reacts as though it is reliving the traumatic events of the past. The body has stored this reaction and, when triggered, returns to what it knows about the past trauma. A woman can reexperience the same level of fear or danger with certain triggers.

In addition, some women are compelled to go back into risky situations. One theory is that there is a desire to master the situation in order to create a different outcome.

All of these things—loss of control, reexperience of the incident, difficulty concentrating, feelings of guilt and shame, negative self-image, depression, disruption in relationships, changes in sexual behavior, fear and anxiety, and high-risk behavior—can often interact with one another, which can cause the overall response to be even more intense. Remember that all these reactions to a traumatic event are normal. Learning more positive ways to cope with trauma is an important part of the healing journey. |

TIME & TOPIC	FACILITATOR NOTES	DISCUSSION WITH WOMEN
48 min. **Exercise:** *The Impact of Violence, Abuse, and Trauma in Your Life* (COLLAGE)	*Bring at least one old magazine and a piece of poster board for each woman; they can share felt pens, glue sticks, and scissors. The magazines need to have pictures and words that reflect the women you are working with, e.g., bilingual and multicultural, if that is appropriate. Have the women cut out words and images that describe the impact of violence, abuse, and/or trauma in their lives and glue them onto the paper in a collage. If scissors are not allowed, such as in a correctional setting, have the women tear out the words and images. Some women will feel more comfortable doing this kind of visual, creative project than others. Explain that people learn and express themselves in different ways and that there is no right or wrong way to do this activity. Just enjoy the time and the experience.* *When the women have completed this exercise, have them share the collages with the group.*	Let's take about twenty-five to thirty minutes to make a collage of words and images that show the impact of violence, abuse, and/or trauma in your life. There is no right or wrong way to do this exercise. We have many magazines that you can cut from as well as felt pens for you to draw with or enhance the magazine pictures. Each person will get a piece of poster board. Please share the scissors and glue sticks. I will let you know when there are about five minutes left. We have some time now to share our collages with one another.
10 min. **Reflection and Homework**	*Discuss.*	What did you learn about the impact of trauma in women's lives?

TIME & TOPIC	FACILITATOR NOTES	DISCUSSION WITH WOMEN
	This may depend on the setting the women are in.	For those of you who did not completely finish your collages, you can add to them during the week. Also, review the trauma chart you did in the last session and see if there is anything you would like to add to it now that we have explored new information about trauma.

Session Notes

MODULE C

Healing from Trauma

MODULE C: SESSION 5

The Addiction and Trauma Connection: Spirals of Recovery and Healing

■ **Time**

1 hour 30 minutes

■ **Session Goal**

Women will understand the addiction/trauma connection.

■ **Participant Learning Objectives**

1. To understand why some women use substances after trauma
2. To understand the spirals of addiction and trauma
3. To learn what emotional and physical safety are
4. To understand the importance of self-care

■ **Session Overview**

- Why Some Women Abuse Substances after Trauma
- The Spiral of Addiction and Recovery
- The Spiral of Trauma and Healing
- *Exercise: Our Own Spirals*
- Safety: A Core Element
- *Exercise: Drawing Safety*
- What Does Self-Care Look Like?
- *Exercise: Self-Care Scale*
- *Reflection and Homework*

■ **Materials and Equipment Needed**

- Easel pad, felt pens, masking tape, crayons
- Participant's workbook
- Cassette or CD player and relaxing music
- VCR and monitor
- Tissues
- *Beyond Trauma* client video

The Addiction and Trauma Connection: Spirals of Recovery and Healing

TIME & TOPIC	FACILITATOR NOTES	DISCUSSION WITH WOMEN
2 min. **Quiet time**		Let us just sit quietly for a few minutes to let ourselves unwind, relax, and turn our attention to where we are now.
10 min. **Check-in**		We'll do our check-in a little differently today by using a weather report as a way to tell each other how we are doing and how we are feeling. If your emotions were weather, what would the weather be today? Bright sunshine? Rain? Mixed sun and clouds? Thunderstorms? Hurricanes?
Goal for the session		Today we are going to look at the similarities between the process of recovery from addiction and the process of healing from trauma.
20 min. **Why some women abuse substances after trauma**	*Discuss and write responses on the easel pad.*	What do you believe are the reasons that some women abuse alcohol and other drugs? Some women use substances to numb the physiological and emotional effects of trauma. Substances can be useful in assisting the survivor to temporarily dissociate or to disconnect the traumatic event from her consciousness. Often women believe that alcohol and other drugs can help them to • make connections with others • comfort themselves • manage or avoid feelings

TIME & TOPIC	FACILITATOR NOTES	DISCUSSION WITH WOMEN
		• escape physical pain
		• ease social withdrawal
		• feel comfortable with sexual intimacy
		• create distance
		• build courage
		• increase hope, make the world seem better
		• forget the past
		• increase a sense of vitality
		• deal with a violent partner
		• dissociate (achieve an altered state)
		• feel numb
		• rewire the brain
		• maintain the status quo
The Spiral of Addiction and Recovery **Video:** *Beyond Trauma* Client video • SPIRALS • GROUP COMMENTS	*Show video: Segment 4.* (Adapted from *Helping Women Recover.* Copyright 1999 by S. Covington. This material is used by permission of John Wiley & Sons, Inc.)	**The Downward Spiral** For many women, there is a connection between substance abuse and trauma and a similarity in how they each work in their lives. We can use a spiral to help demonstrate this. First we'll look at the process of addiction. Let's look at page 28 in the workbook.

Spiral of Addiction and Recovery
(Transformation)

Upward Spiral

Downward Spiral

Addiction
(Constriction)

Recovery
(Expansion) |

TIME & TOPIC	FACILITATOR NOTES	DISCUSSION WITH WOMEN
		There are two parts to the spiral. One part is a path that goes downward, representing a woman's life as addiction takes hold. The path is not always a straight line, but rather is revolving and circular as it goes along in one direction. At the bottom of the downward spiral, there is a turning point. This is where a woman steps onto a new path—recovery. This new path moves upward and represents the woman's recovery from the addiction.
	Draw a downward spiral on the easel pad.	The downward spiral of addiction revolves around the object of addiction, such as alcohol, marijuana, and other drugs. The object of the addiction is shown by the line that goes through the middle of the spiral and is ever-present in the woman's life. The process of addiction pulls the addict into tighter and tighter circles along this path, constricting her life, isolating her from others, and limiting healthy activities until she is completely focused on the drug. The object of her addiction becomes the organizing principle of her life. Using alcohol or other drugs, protecting her supply, hiding her addiction from others, and cultivating her love-hate relationship with her drug begin to interfere in her world and constrict her life.
		For women, addiction is particularly hard since society's double standard inflicts far more shame on a woman for having an addiction than it does on a man.
	Discuss.	What are some of the labels given to women who are alcoholics or addicts?
		The labels may include *slut, lush, unfit mother,* and so on. Although society may stigmatize a male addict as a "bum," it rarely attacks his sexuality or his competence as

TIME & TOPIC	FACILITATOR NOTES	DISCUSSION WITH WOMEN
	Draw an upward spiral.	a parent. A woman who enters treatment may come with a heavy burden of shame. Women's recovery from addiction can be viewed as an upward spiral. A woman's choices, life options, and opportunities expand when she stops using alcohol or other drugs. Her world is broadened, and the drug does not have the grip around her daily decisions. The upward spiral of recovery revolves around the drug in wider and wider circles as the addiction loosens its grip and the woman's world opens up. Her world grows to include healthy relations, an expanded self-concept, and a richer sexual and spiritual life. It is a time for change, growth, opportunity, and expansion. One way of thinking about addiction is as "a chronic neglect of self in favor of something or someone else" (Covington 1999, 16). So, how does an addicted woman shift from this chronic neglect of self to a healthy care of self? How does this woman get from the downward spiral (constriction) to the upward, ever-widening spiral (expansion and growth)? How does a woman grow, recover, and get her life on a healthy course? In the next section, we will explore these questions further.
The Spiral of Trauma and Healing		Now let us use the same concept of a spiral and apply it to trauma. As we talked about in an earlier session, trauma often constricts and limits a woman's life. The traumatic event(s) in her life often become a central issue for her (as represented by the line through the middle of the downward spiral). Again, there is a turning point at the bottom of the downward spiral. The upward spiral can also represent the process of healing

TIME & TOPIC	FACILITATOR NOTES	DISCUSSION WITH WOMEN
		from trauma. As a woman becomes more aware of how trauma has impacted her life, she experiences less constriction and limitation. With new behaviors and coping skills, there is greater opportunity for growth and expansion. While the trauma is still a thread that runs through her life, it is no longer the central focus.
	(Adapted from *Helping Women Recover*. Copyright 1999 by S. Covington. This material is used by permission of John Wiley & Sons, Inc.)	**Spiral of Trauma and Healing** (Transformation) Upward Spiral Downward Spiral **Trauma** (Constriction) **Healing** (Expansion)
15 min. **Exercise:** *Our Own Spirals*		Again, let us take a look at the workbook. On page 30, you will notice that there is space for you to list all of the things that 1. constrict (limit or restrict) your life. If you have an addiction, how has that constricted your life? How has trauma constricted your life? 2. expand your life. What are the things in your life that can help you grow and expand and recover? We will take about three to five minutes for you to write down your ideas.

TIME & TOPIC	FACILITATOR NOTES	DISCUSSION WITH WOMEN
	After three to five minutes, either use the spiral you just drew or draw another spiral on the easel pad and ask the women to identify where they feel they are on the spiral. Some may feel comfortable speaking aloud about where they are on the spiral, while others may not. Have women brainstorm and share while you write responses on the easel pad.	Where do you think you are on the spiral?
	Discuss.	I would like you to pick one constriction issue to work on. Think about your life and that constriction. What will it take to make that constriction change and begin to open up the spiral toward expansion? Write your ideas on page 31 of the workbook.
	Discuss.	Now let us go back to the questions I mentioned a few minutes ago. How do you think a woman shifts from chronic neglect of self—often sparked by a life trauma—to healthy care of self (e.g., eating and sleeping, creating a safe environment, developing a support system)? How does a woman shift from constriction to expansion and growth (e.g., moves out of abusive relationship, expands support system, creates and uses opportunities, researches community resources)? How does a woman grow and recover?

TIME & TOPIC	FACILITATOR NOTES	DISCUSSION WITH WOMEN
18 min. **Safety: A core element**		Now let's take a look at what a woman needs to do to begin the process of healing from trauma. As we learned before, safety is the first step and a core element in healing from trauma. This includes both physical and emotional safety. Safety is so important that we will be referring to it throughout our sessions.
	Discuss. Typical responses include the following: lock doors; do not go out at night alone; do not accept drinks from unknown people; carry a cellular phone; go to a friend's house when home doesn't feel safe.	What are some things women do to feel safe in their lives?
	Discuss. Typical responses include the following: being around people who won't hurt me or play games with my mind; having a good friend to call if I need her; being around people who support and love me.	What is emotional safety?
	Discuss. Typical responses include the following: in my car when I am driving; hugging my kids; in my home, in my bed with the doors locked and porch light on.	When and where do you feel emotionally safe?
	Discuss. Typical responses include the following: at my parents' house; around people who have been drinking or doing drugs; around men.	When and where do you feel emotionally unsafe?

TIME & TOPIC	FACILITATOR NOTES	DISCUSSION WITH WOMEN
	Discuss. Typical responses include the following: being far away from a person who can abuse me; being in a safe environment like a women's shelter; being with friends or with family; having a safe place to go. *Keep in mind that there is no right or wrong answer. Each woman is unique in her feelings about safety.*	What is physical safety? What do you do to keep yourself physically safe?
Exercise: *Drawing Safety*	*Distribute equal varieties of crayons or place them all on a table so that the women can take what they like.*	Please turn to page 33 in your workbooks.
	Give the instructions slowly, in a calming way. (Remember, some women may need to keep their eyes open.)	Close your eyes. . . . Relax. . . . Breathe deeply and slowly. . . . Begin to focus and think back to a time or place when you felt safe—or if you cannot think of a safe place, then to a time or place where you were least afraid. Think about the sights, the sounds, and the smells. What would the colors be? What made you feel safe? Relax and just enjoy where you are. Slowly begin to open your eyes.
	Allow five to seven minutes for the women to draw.	Please begin to draw what came to your mind—images, feelings, thoughts. Your drawing does not have to be artistic; just draw what safety means to you. Now let's share our drawings with each other. As you show your drawing, please tell us about it.

TIME & TOPIC	FACILITATOR NOTES	DISCUSSION WITH WOMEN
15 min. **What does self-care look like?**		We have been discussing safety, particularly safety with others. A key part of safety that we often overlook is safety with ourselves. One way we develop safety with ourselves is through self-care. Self-care is a range of behaviors that includes everything from what we eat and personal hygiene to valuing ourselves and acknowledging our feelings. How we take care of ourselves is very important. When we are doing a good job of caring for ourselves, we are at less risk for self-destructive behavior. What does self-care look like? Often women who have been abused do not know how to focus on their own needs.
Exercise: *Self-Care Scale*		On pages 34–35 in your workbook, you will find a scale that is designed to help you see areas in which you are already taking care of yourself. It also helps you see areas that you might be neglecting and areas that you might want to continue to work on in the future. It is not a test. There are no right or wrong answers, nor is this a way to measure yourself against others. This is just for you. (scale shown on next page)

TIME & TOPIC	FACILITATOR NOTES	DISCUSSION WITH WOMEN
		�苗 E X E R C I S E **SELF-CARE SCALE** Please take a few moments to look at the following fifteen items and determine the degree to which you do the following. Put an X on the line to show where you think you are on the scale. This is only for you to see, and no one will judge how well you are doing. Not at all Just a little Pretty much Very much 1. I keep up my physical appearance (nails, hair, bathing, clean clothes). 2. I exercise regularly. 3. I eat healthy meals. 4. I get restful sleep. 5. I go to work/school (or complete tasks). 6. I can adapt to change. 7. I keep up my living space. 8. I take constructive criticism well. 9. I can accept praise. 10. I laugh at funny things. 11. I acknowledge my needs and feelings. 12. I engage in new interests. 13. I can relax without drugs and alcohol. 14. I value myself. 15. I live a clean and sober life.
	(Adapted from *Helping Women Recover.* Copyright 1999 by S. Covington. This material is used by permission of John Wiley & Sons, Inc.)	
	Discuss when everyone has completed the scale.	Take about five minutes to fill out the scale. You will notice it lists various tasks related to self. Please respond to each of the scale items in terms of how you act now and what your life is like now. Remember, this is not a test. It is a tool you can use to see areas in which you are caring for yourself effectively and areas you may want to work on.

TIME & TOPIC	FACILITATOR NOTES	DISCUSSION WITH WOMEN
10 min. **Reflection and Homework**		Think back to the exercises we used in this session. In the future, you can use • the weather report technique to check in with yourself • the spirals of addiction and trauma to pinpoint your place in the healing journey • the Self-Care Scale They are all things that you can use whenever you need them. They are all available to you as tools. Your homework assignment is to focus on self-care, identifying the obstacles to self-care and the areas of self-care you would like to enhance in your own life. See if there is one area of self-care that needs attention and that you would like to do some work on. Over the next few days, be aware of your environment and what makes you feel safe, comfortable, secure, and supported.

Session Notes

MODULE C: SESSION 6

Grounding and Self-Soothing

■ Time

1 hour 30 minutes

■ Session Goal

Women will develop the ability to ground and soothe themselves.

■ Participant Learning Objectives

1. To understand what feeling grounded means
2. To learn grounding exercises
3. To learn self-soothing exercises

■ Session Overview

• What Does It Mean to "Feel Grounded"?
• *Exercise: Grounding*
• *Exercise: Self-Soothing Chart*
• *Exercise: Relaxation*
• Developing Personal Boundaries
• *Exercise: Physical Boundaries*
• *Reflection and Homework*

■ Materials and Equipment Needed

• Easel pad, felt pens, masking tape
• Cassette or CD player and relaxing music
• Participant's workbook
• Tissues

Grounding and Self-Soothing

TIME & TOPIC	FACILITATOR NOTES	DISCUSSION WITH WOMEN
2 min. **Quiet time**		Let us just sit quietly for a few minutes to let ourselves unwind, relax, and turn our attention to where we are now.
10 min. **Check-in**	*Discuss.*	When we last got together, we talked about the Self-Care Scale. I hope you had some time since our last session to think about your own self-care. What is one thing that you did for yourself this week that is self-care?
Goal for the session		Today we are going to focus on how to ground and soothe ourselves.
40 min. **What does it mean to "feel grounded"?**	*Discuss.*	What does it mean to you to feel "centered" or "grounded"? In an earlier session, we talked about grounding techniques as ways to detach or disconnect from inner emotional discomfort by focusing on the outer world. Grounding techniques are also strategies to help a person who is dissociating (emotionally absent) "come back" into current reality and feelings. Grounding techniques help the person become aware of the here and now. When a woman is dissociating or having a flashback, she may feel like she is watching a movie in her mind, as flashes or clips of past memories appear. Grounding techniques can help women realize that they are in the here and

TIME & TOPIC	FACILITATOR NOTES	DISCUSSION WITH WOMEN
		now and what they are experiencing is in the past—it is not happening now. When you experience trauma, you may lose your grounding and centering. It is important to reestablish your ground so you cannot be easily knocked off balance by your emotions and your reactions to the trauma. Here are several grounding and centering exercises that help support deeper insight and resolution of trauma symptoms. Do these exercises slowly and respectfully. If at any time you find an exercise disturbing or feel emotions build up inside of you, stop and let things settle; then try to continue with the exercise. There will be an opportunity at the end of each exercise for discussion.
Exercise: *Grounding*	*Have the women stand in a circle.* *Discuss.*	**Exercise 1** Stand and feel your feet on the ground. Notice the springiness in your legs. Feel the way your feet connect with the ground, almost like a magnet is holding you there or a tree with big, strong roots. With your feet firmly planted, sway slowly from side to side from the ankles, then forward and backward. This will help you find your center of gravity. It is usually located in the upper pelvic area. As you continue to sway, place your hands on your lower belly and sense your center of gravity. Now, sit back in your chair. Relax. Be sure that your feet are firmly on the ground. Place your hands on your lower belly again and feel the energy coming into that area through your feet. What do you feel?

TIME & TOPIC	FACILITATOR NOTES	DISCUSSION WITH WOMEN
	Discuss.	**Exercise 2** Another exercise is "belly breathing." Lie on your back (or you can sit in a chair) with one hand on your chest and one on your stomach. Most people find that they primarily breathe from their chest. You can tell when your hand on your chest moves up and down. Try moving your breath deeper into your lower belly so that your hand on your stomach begins to move up and down. Blow the air out of your mouth, rather than your nose, and let your belly fill with air.
	Discuss.	**Exercise 3** Sit in a comfortable position with your feet on the floor. Concentrate on your breathing—the breathing in, the pause, the breathing out. Feel your body expand from the center and release back toward the center. With each breath, breathe a little deeper, moving deeper down into your abdomen. As you breathe in, take in "good things" (self-love, hope, courage, joy), and as you breathe out, let go of things you do not want in your life (self-criticism, stress, fear). Do this for two to three minutes.
	Discuss.	**Exercise 4** Another way to feel grounded and centered is to walk without shoes, if weather and terrain permit (this may or may not be permissible in a correctional setting). In the park, in the woods, on the beach, on your favorite street, in your garden, or on the grass in your yard can all be good places to try this out. Breathe deeply and think about your feet as they connect with the ground. Look around and take in your surroundings. Be in the present and feel the connection with your world.

TIME & TOPIC	FACILITATOR NOTES	DISCUSSION WITH WOMEN
	Discuss.	**Other Exercises** What are some other ways you can feel grounded and centered? Some people feel grounded holding or lying down with an animal and listening to its heartbeat or the calmness in its breathing. Some find a grounded feeling by looking up at the large, vast sky and watching the clouds go by. Others find it in walking through nature and connecting with the universe through their feet as well as their senses. When we are working through painful things, such as a past trauma, it's important to have ways to comfort or soothe ourselves without using alcohol or other drugs. It is helpful to know ways to comfort yourself without relying on temporary fixes that may, in fact, complicate your life even more.
Exercise: *Self-Soothing Chart*	*Have the women brainstorm some self-soothing techniques. Write ideas on the easel pad. Try to elicit at least two or three ideas from each person when you brainstorm.* *Examples might include taking a long, hot shower, taking a walk and thinking, talking to a trusted friend, writing in a journal, sewing, reading, playing relaxing music while lying on your back on the floor with your eyes closed, exercising, painting, writing down the words you want to say to someone, doing yoga, meditation, and deep breathing.*	In earlier sessions, we talked about a technique called "self-soothing." There is no one way to self-soothe since each person is unique. In fact, you have probably used various ways to self-soothe during these sessions. Let us explore more techniques and help discover what works best for you. In your workbook, you will find a Self-Soothing Chart on page 40. <table><tr><td></td><td>ALONE</td><td>WITH OTHERS</td></tr><tr><td>Daytime</td><td></td><td></td></tr><tr><td>Nighttime</td><td></td><td></td></tr></table> (Adapted from *Helping Women Recover*. Copyright 1999 by S. Covington. This material is used by permission of John Wiley & Sons, Inc.)

TIME & TOPIC	FACILITATOR NOTES	DISCUSSION WITH WOMEN
	Some women find eating or buying something can be self-soothing. However, these methods can be addictive in themselves. In criminal justice settings, you will need to help the women find suitable self-soothing techniques, since many of the previous options are not available to them. These might include reading, crocheting, writing in a journal, or meditating.	Feel free to take notes and put them in the appropriate boxes as we discuss ways to self-soothe. We all need a variety of strategies to soothe ourselves that are appropriate for the situation. Consequently, you will find four boxes on the chart. For instance, one strategy might work when we are with others (such as at work or school) but not when we are at home alone, and vice versa. Some things will work during the night but not during the day. So, we need ways to soothe ourselves in all four circumstances: alone or with others during the night and alone or with others during the day.
	Discuss. Try to get at least two to three responses from the group.	Let's look at the box in the upper left-hand corner of the worksheet. What are some things you do to self-soothe (to calm and relax yourself) when you are alone in the daytime?
	Discuss.	What are some things you do to self-soothe when alone in the nighttime?
	Discuss.	What are some things you do to self-soothe during the day when you are with others?
	Discuss.	What are some things you do to relax or calm yourself when you are with others in the nighttime?
		The importance of self-soothing is to feel grounded and centered. Learning how to calm yourself and relax when you have been bombarded by intense emotions is a self-soothing skill we all need to develop. It can be very individual and a good way to take care of yourself.

TIME & TOPIC	FACILITATOR NOTES	DISCUSSION WITH WOMEN
Exercise: *Relaxation*	*Remember, some women may need to keep their eyes open.* *Use a soft, melodic tone of voice.* *Pause.*	Relaxation is one of the best ways to self-soothe. One way to relax is to get off of your feet. You may lie down on your back on the floor or sit, if you would prefer. Now, close your eyes. Take a deep breath in while you silently count to four: one . . . two . . . three . . . four. Now begin breathing out slowly: one . . . two . . . three . . . four. Try to breathe deeply from within your abdomen, rather than higher in your chest. Breathe in again and now out again. Let's repeat that slow breathing a couple more times. Now, in your mind, I want you to picture your favorite safe place to be. Maybe you are walking in a beautiful park or garden. Maybe you are getting cozy in your favorite chair or in your bed. Maybe you are lying in the sun or boating on the water. Picture that place in your mind and imagine yourself there. Keep breathing deeply and very slowly. Starting with your head and working down your body like a scan, let your muscles relax. Let your forehead relax. Let your cheekbones relax. Let your jaw joints relax. Let your neck and upper shoulders relax. As you exhale, imagine all the tension going out with each breath. Let it go. Let your hands and arms go limp next to you. Let your chest, stomach, and whole middle part of your body relax. Keep breathing in and out. Let your hips, your buttocks, and your upper legs and lower legs relax. Let your feet and toes relax. Let your whole body relax. Breathe in and out. Keep imagining that safe place you selected. Enjoy where you are; enjoy the tension going out of your body. Be relaxed, almost floating and weightless, as you stay in that image.

TIME & TOPIC	FACILITATOR NOTES	DISCUSSION WITH WOMEN
	Discuss.	Now open your eyes. How do you feel right now? Do you feel more relaxed? Breathing deeply is a simple and easy way to feel less stressed or anxious. Letting your breath help you release the anxiety in your body is an important skill for self-care.
30 min. **Developing personal boundaries**	*Discuss.*	Another skill that helps a woman feel centered and grounded, and more in control of her life, is developing boundaries. What do we mean when we talk about "personal boundaries"? I think most of us have had the experience of feeling that someone is standing too close to us—or that his or her face is too close to us. We feel like this person is "in our face" and has crossed our physcial boundary. When a woman is abused, it is a boundary violation: Her physical, sexual, and emotional boundaries are not respected and are crossed. When women's boundaries have been violated and disrupted, we have difficulty with our boundaries with others. If a child has been sexually abused, there is a risk that she will have difficulty knowing what is sexually appropriate or inappropriate in her adolescent and adult life. In order to create a strong, caring relationship, it is important for each person not only to know when and how to set clear limits, but also to accept and honor the boundaries and limits set by other people. Personal boundaries are based on our upbringing, our culture, and our experience with others. It can be empowering to set and regulate your own boundaries, but it is not always easy to do so.

TIME & TOPIC	FACILITATOR NOTES	DISCUSSION WITH WOMEN
		When we are caught unprepared, we may over- or underreact. Communicating clearly what your limits are with strangers, family members, or friends is an important first step. Other people cannot guess your boundaries. Some people will try to test them or use their own comfort level as the standard for yours. Therefore, it is important to tell them when you feel comfortable or uncomfortable. It is best to determine your boundaries on your own internal compass, not on your reaction to external things or people. One way to think about boundaries is like "zippers." Imagine that you have a zipper around you. When the zipper tab is on the outside, others can move it at will. If it is on the inside, you can control it.
Exercise: *Physical Boundaries*	*If yours is a small group, do not divide into pairs but have the women do this exercise in the full group, two at a time.* *Pause while the pairs do this activity.* *Pause while the pairs do this activity. Then have them switch roles so that each woman has the experience of creating her physical boundaries.*	For this exercise, you will pair up with another woman and spread out around the room. Now stand still and face each other, standing about six to eight feet apart. One of you, while maintaining eye contact, will silently motion to the other to move closer and then indicate "stop" with your hand when your partner is close enough for comfort. While the first woman is still facing straight ahead, the other woman repeats the exercise from all directions (left side, right side, and back). The one standing still raises her hand when she feels the other is close enough. You have just created your personal physical boundary—that bubble around you where you feel most safe and comfortable.

TIME & TOPIC	FACILITATOR NOTES	DISCUSSION WITH WOMEN
	Discuss. One example might be: "Some women have three inches of personal space while some have four feet." *Discuss.*	What are the differences among the people around the room in terms of personal boundaries? How do you feel when someone gets too close to you? Are there differences when this person is someone you don't know or a friend? Differences if this person is a man or a woman? Are there cultural differences?
8 min. **Reflection and Homework**		What is one thing that you have learned about yourself today? Between now and our next session, think about your personal boundaries. Remember situations where you felt comfortable and times when you felt uncomfortable in terms of your boundaries. Also, I want you to try some grounding and self-soothing exercises. Pay attention to how you feel before and after each exercise. Record it in your workbook. At our next session, we will discuss what worked for you and what did not work. Everyone is unique, and some exercises will work better for you than others.
	This may not be possible in residential programs or correctional institutions.	If you have a photograph of yourself as a young girl (one to ten years old), please bring it to our next session.

Abuse and the Family

■ **Time**

1 hour 30 minutes

■ **Session Goal**

Women will recognize the dynamics and understand the impact of abuse in families.

■ **Participant Learning Objectives**

1. To understand how family dynamics influence or impact children
2. To increase women's awareness and understanding of abuse in families
3. To identify the little girl/child within

■ **Session Overview**

- *Exercise: Family Sculpture*
- Abuse in Families
- The Little Girl/Child Inside
- *Exercise: Getting to Know My Inner Child*
- *Reflection and Homework*

■ **Materials and Equipment Needed**

- Easel pad, felt pens, masking tape
- Participant's workbook
- Cassette or CD player and relaxing music
- VCR and monitor
- Tissues
- *Beyond Trauma* client video

Abuse and the Family

TIME & TOPIC	FACILITATOR NOTES	DISCUSSION WITH WOMEN
2 min. **Quiet time**		Let us just sit quietly for a few minutes to let ourselves unwind, relax, and turn our attention to where we are now.
10 min. **Check-in**	*Fill out the Self-Soothing Chart with the group— what worked best during the week?*	Would anyone like to share a self-soothing or grounding exercise you did since our last group session?
Goal for the session		Today we will focus on recognizing the dynamics and understanding the impact of abuse in families.
50 min. **Exercise:** *Family Sculpture* **Video:** *Beyond Trauma* Client video • FAMILY SCULPTURE	*As facilitator, you have the option of showing the video of the family sculpture exercise and discussing it, or doing the exercise with the group.* *Show video: Segment 5.* *Some of the women in the group come from families in which their needs were not met. They took on roles in an effort to survive in emotionally confusing environments and to get their basic needs met. Roles in dysfunctional families typically are rigid. Family members try to manage their feelings of*	In this session, we are looking at families: how they function, our roles in our families, and how our families have shaped who we are in the world. What do families look like? Let us take a look at one family through a process known as creating a "family sculpture." The role or roles a child is given in his or her family is one of the major forces that shapes who the child becomes. Roles in the family help children begin to define their personal boundaries. If children's boundaries are violated in the family, such as from abuse, it can be difficult for children to develop a strong sense of self.

TIME & TOPIC	FACILITATOR NOTES	DISCUSSION WITH WOMEN
	confusion and low self-esteem by hiding behind clearly defined and predictable roles. In abusive homes, children may try to become invisible in order to avoid punishment; the mask of an approved role is an attempt to create a protective cover. "Assigned" roles limit the free range of human expression. They diminish a person's ability to feel or listen to internal cues since roles are a response to external cues. The primary function of a family structure is to meet growing children's needs. One of the characteristics that set troubled families apart from healthy ones is their reversal of this mission. They expect the children to meet the needs of the adults (such as taking on roles and tasks inappropriate for their age), to serve the family, to live in denial, and to hide true feelings. *The instructions for the group exercise are at the right.*	**Family Sculpture Exercise** Relationships help form who we are. Our early relationships in our families helped us establish patterns of how we view ourselves and relate to the world and others. It's easier to understand family relationships when you can see them, so I am going to build a "family sculpture" using volunteers from our group. I will place some of you in positions in the sculpture and build a sample

TIME & TOPIC	FACILITATOR NOTES	DISCUSSION WITH WOMEN
		family. You will have a chance to talk about how your family was similar or different.
		You may find that you experience strong feelings when we do this exercise. So please respect any emotions that you or other group members may show. This is how we begin to understand our past so we can begin our healing journey to build a positive future.
		None of us had a "Leave It to Beaver" family. Your family may not have had a father, mother, and four kids. For this exercise, I am going to sculpt a family with two parents and four children, but that is just for illustration.
	Have the volunteers come up to the front.	I need six volunteers to participate in my sculpture, which will represent a family with an addiction problem.
	Ask the volunteer to stand next to the facilitator.	We are going to start with the father as the addicted person. We know that many families do not have fathers, or that the mother may have the addiction, but this is a simple way to start thinking about family. Who is willing to play the role of the father?
		This man might be the real father of the kids in this family or a stepfather or the mother's boyfriend. We will call him the "father" for simplicity.
	Help the father stand on a chair facing the group. Be sure the chair is safe and sturdy.	The father in this family is standing on a chair to symbolize three things: (1) Power. This father puts himself above the others in the family, and the family members may do the same. (2) Lack of attention. The chair represents something that takes the father's attention away from the needs of the family. It might be alcohol and other drugs, it might be his work, it might be TV or fishing or hanging out with buddies, it might be a crime, or it might be an affair. It could be

TIME & TOPIC	FACILITATOR NOTES	DISCUSSION WITH WOMEN
		any addiction or preoccupation that pulls his attention away from the needs of others. (3) Disconnection. Standing on a chair symbolizes disconnect from the earth—literally and figuratively—with the father becoming ungrounded, which happens with addictions and preoccupations.
	Say to the father: *Allow the father to make up an answer, such as "bourbon." On a piece of paper, draw an outline of a bottle and tape it to the back wall. Or pick an object in the room for the person to focus on.*	Let us say your preoccupation is addiction. What is your favorite drug or drink?
	Say to the father:	Look at the bottle taped on the back wall and stay focused on it. This is your obsession. It is always on your mind.
	Get someone to volunteer to be the mother and to stand on the ground next to the father, who is on the chair.	
	Say to the mother: *The usual response is "no."*	Do you feel close and connected to your partner?
	Say to the women in the group:	We want to feel connected in relationships. But because this woman's partner is preoccupied with something, or because the power between them is unequal, she feels disconnected.
	Say to the mother: *The mother will usually answer, "nothing," because she feels shame or the need*	Look out at the group and imagine your family and friends. What do you want your family and friends to know about your partner's alcoholism?

TIME & TOPIC	FACILITATOR NOTES	DISCUSSION WITH WOMEN
	for secrecy to protect their reputation. If she wants to tell about the alcohol problem, ask her to proceed with what she would say to her friends, parents, or colleagues. This usually leaves her silent. She does not know what to say. Ask the mother to step in front of the chair.	
	Say to the mother: *The usual response is "everything is fine."*	You are now standing in front of your partner's chair to cover up his addiction or dysfunction. Now, what do you want your family and friends to know about your relationship?
	Say to the mother:	I want you to smile so that people will think that everything is fine in your relationship. Keep smiling. Never stop smiling.
	Stand behind the chair. Partway through the dialogue, start shaking the chair a little. Be careful not to cause the person to fall.	Notice how the father starts to lean on the mother in order to feel more stable. He maintains his stability by holding on to the mother's shoulders.
	Say to the father: *The usual response is "I feel better" or "safer."*	How does that feel, holding your partner's shoulders?
	Say to the mother: *The usual response is "yes."*	Do you feel more connected to your partner now than you did when you were standing next to him?
	Ask the mother to step forward three or four steps. She probably will stop and step back in order to keep the father from falling, because he is leaning on her	

TIME & TOPIC	FACILITATOR NOTES	DISCUSSION WITH WOMEN
	shoulders and might fall. The father will have to stretch or reach out in order to keep connected to the mother.	
	Say to the mother: *Mother's response is that she thinks of his concerns, safety, and well-being, not of herself. She feels she needs to step back closer to keep her partner from falling.*	What if you were considering ending the relationship or branching out into the world more? How does it feel when you step away while your partner is leaning on you?
	Say to the father: *Father's usual answer is "it is better when she is close."*	Which feels better: having her step away or having her stay close to you?
	Say to the women in the group: *Have the mother and father remain in their positions.*	It is normal to seek comfort and stability. Sometimes maintaining the status quo in a family is perceived as easier. As women, we reorganize our lives to stay connected even if it is uncomfortable for us. If our partner is drinking or using drugs, we may drink or use drugs in order to stay connected. We may stay connected by sharing other activities, such as going to a bar and drinking or watching television and using drugs together.
	Say to the volunteers:	Who would like to play the role of the oldest child in this family?
	Direct this oldest child to stand to the right of the mother and father.	All children want to feel safe and loved in their families. In a family like this one, the children take on roles to survive, keep tranquility, and be accepted in their families. The family is supposed to meet the children's needs. In unhealthy families, the children often exist to meet the adults' needs.

TIME & TOPIC	FACILITATOR NOTES	DISCUSSION WITH WOMEN
		The oldest, or firstborn, child is often the Hero Child. She has all the privileges of an only child for a while until other siblings come along. When a brother or sister is born, at first she may feel threatened but then looks for ways to win back her parents' attention and approval. She may try to follow all the rules perfectly. The more unstable the home life becomes, the more she will overachieve and be super-responsible to keep the family together. The Hero Child often gets good grades and excels in activities. Her behavior is a way for her to control life around her.
	Say to the Hero Child: *The Hero Child's response is that she feels good about her mother. Ask the Hero Child to link arms with the mother.*	Imagine that you come home from school every day, having done well in everything. Tell your mother all about how great you are doing. How do you feel about your mother?
	Say to the Hero Child: *The Hero Child's usual response is that her father seems uninvolved and disconnected.*	How do you feel about your father up there?
	Say to the Hero Child: *The Hero Child may say that she feels angry toward the father. Ask the Hero Child to point her finger at the father to show that she feels angry.*	How do you feel about that?
	Say to the Hero Child: *The Hero Child's usual response is that she wants outsiders to think that everything at home is "just fine" or even perfect.*	Now, what do you want the kids at school to know about your family?

TIME & TOPIC	FACILITATOR NOTES	DISCUSSION WITH WOMEN
	Say to the Hero Child:	Okay, if everything is fine, then smile. Keep smiling so that everyone will know that your family is fine.
	Say to the volunteers: *Direct the second-born child (the Scapegoat) to stand to the left of and apart from the family, but still facing the group.*	Who would like to volunteer to be the second-born child?
	Say to the Scapegoat: *Direct the Scapegoat to cross her arms with an attitude that says, "You can't tell me what to do."*	Can you compete with the Hero Child in your family? No. If you are going to get any attention, you will probably need to make your connection in your own way and probably with the kids at school rather than at home.
	Say to the women in the group:	The second child might be called the Scapegoat and gets attention at home only from acting out. Sometimes the child deliberately causes trouble just to escape boredom. She relieves stress in the family by taking attention away from the issues between the mother and father that they are not addressing. So, everyone pretends that the real family problem is the Scapegoat. Because of this acting out, the Scapegoat may be at risk for physical abuse by parents, school officials, or other authority figures. She is more likely to skip school, get pregnant, shoplift, or use drugs or alcohol at home. She may withdraw or act disengaged.
	Say to the volunteers: *Direct the Lost Child to stand apart from and behind the family, with her back to the group.*	Who would like to volunteer to play child number three, the Lost Child?

TIME & TOPIC	FACILITATOR NOTES	DISCUSSION WITH WOMEN
	Say to the Lost Child:	Can you connect with the family? No, not with your parents, not with your perfect Hero Child sibling, and not with your wild Scapegoat sibling. You are on your own, floating and feeling lost.
	Say to the women in the group:	This child turns her back on the family altogether. She stays home and does quiet activities (like reading) or hangs out alone, losing herself in television, the computer, or video games. She lives in a world of imagination. In a healthy family, a third child might learn to compete and excel in something uniquely her own. But in a high-stress family like this one, the Lost Child often is at high risk for sexual abuse because she is vulnerable and isolated.
	Say to the volunteers:	Who would like to volunteer to play child number four, the Mascot?
	Say to the women in the group:	This is the fourth child, the Mascot.
	Direct the Mascot to bounce around the family members, pulling on the mother and father and then jumping away. The Mascot child always keeps moving.	
	Say to the women in the group:	In healthy families, the youngest child is often the most relaxed and cheerful. Parents may have eased up on their child-rearing methods by this time. This child has plenty of opportunities to play with brothers and sisters. But in a troubled home, each additional child adds more stress to the family. With more kids, each child has more difficulty getting the parents' attention, especially since there is tremendous energy being taken by the addicted parent. So the

TIME & TOPIC	FACILITATOR NOTES	DISCUSSION WITH WOMEN
		role of the fourth child is that of family Mascot. She will do anything to attract attention through humor, charm, or hyper-activity. This, too, takes the focus off the tension between the mother and father, relieving family stress. The hyperactive Mascot, as well as the Scapegoat, may be at high risk for physical abuse. Each child has a role that contributes something to the family's survival. The Hero Child gives the family self-esteem. The Scapegoat acts out the family's pain. The Lost Child takes care of herself, asks for nothing, and is almost invisible. The Mascot is a pressure valve that relieves the family's stress.
	The key points here are that this is a high-stress, high-tension family. The family is organized around the addicted person.	
	Ask the father to step off the chair—carefully. Ask the mother to carefully step onto the chair and stare off into the distance. Ask the father to stand in front of the mother, and direct the mother to lean on the father.	This is just one example of a troubled family. The scenario could have easily switched with the mother having the addiction.
	Ask the father to wander away from the mother a few steps to show that he is distracted from the family by something. *Also have the group look at the family dynamics of a single-parent family in which the mother is a substance user.*	What often happens when the mother has an addiction is that the father will find something outside the family to distract him, such as an affair or long hours at work. He will not necessarily divorce her, but he will cease to be an emotionally present partner, someone the mother can lean on. If that happens, the family will need the Hero Child to step into the parental role and be the person that the addict mother can lean on. Typically, when fathers are substance abusers, mothers become overly

TIME & TOPIC	FACILITATOR NOTES	DISCUSSION WITH WOMEN
		involved in their kids' lives. However, when mothers are substance abusers, fathers usually do not become overly involved and may let one of the older kids take on the parenting role. Or, there may not be a father in this family.
	Ask the Hero Child to step in front of the chair so that the mother can lean on her. Ask the mother to lean on the Hero Child.	So, the Hero Child now plays the role of the parent. Sometimes if the father abuses substances, the mother will have her emotional needs met through her oldest child in an incestuous way, even if the incest is not physical. Sometimes fathers will do this with Hero children.
		The Scapegoat and Mascot are at risk of physical abuse. The Hero and Lost Child are at risk of sexual abuse. The mother is at risk of domestic violence. All family members are at risk of emotional abuse; it is not safe to have or share feelings. Each role a child plays in a troubled family comes with its own vulnerability to abuse.
		Why are we looking at these family dynamics? These roles were important to our survival as children. Yet most of us carry the roles into adulthood, even though they have outlived their usefulness and may have little connection to who we are now. These roles can be another form of constriction, in addition to the constriction of gender expectations, trauma, and addiction.
	Ask the volunteers in the sculpture exercise to leave their positions and go back to their chairs in the circle.	Let us give our family members a round of applause for their volunteering. It is not easy to look at our past, but it helps us take charge of and change our future.

TIME & TOPIC	FACILITATOR NOTES	DISCUSSION WITH WOMEN
Debrief family sculpture exercise	*Some women will feel sadness and shame about their own parenting after seeing how an addicted parent affects a family sculpture.* *Empower the women by saying that as they become more conscious along the healing journey, they will be more able to choose to raise their children in healthy ways.* *Explain that it is important for women to focus right now on what they learned about parenting from their own parents, and then they will see what they want to do the same or differently with their own children.*	Let us debrief what we just experienced. Now that we have looked at this family with two parents and four children (and a single-parent family), does anyone have questions about how this plays out in different kinds of families or in their own family? Here are some dynamics from other kinds of families: **Single Child** A single child in a troubled family often moves among the roles and carries the weight of the family's problems. Single children tend to become isolated because they have no siblings with whom to bond. **Single Parent** If the family is a single-parent family and that parent abuses substances, usually the oldest child—or the oldest daughter—takes over the parent role and responsibilities. **Hero Child but Not the First Born** If there is a large gap in age between siblings, any child may become the Hero Child. Sometimes the sexes of the children affect who takes what role (e.g., daughters are never the Heroes in some families).

TIME & TOPIC	FACILITATOR NOTES	DISCUSSION WITH WOMEN
Abuse in families		Many women do not know that they have been abused because they assume their family is normal. Domestic violence is one type of abuse that is defined as any exploitive or threatening behaviors intended to harm or exert power over another family or household member. We can see in our sculpture when and how the mother was at risk for abuse.

The important indicators for abuse in the family are behaviors that either threaten or use people, with the intent to harm, control, or exert power over others.

Let us talk a little more in depth about sexual abuse in families. This is the Sexual Abuse in Families continuum. |
| | *Draw a horizontal line on the easel pad. On the far left end, write "psychological abuse"; in the middle of the line, write "covert abuse"; and at the far right end, write "overt abuse."* | **Sexual Abuse in Families**

⟶

Psychological Abuse   Covert Abuse   Overt Abuse |
| | *Examples include sexual jokes, verbal harassment, violating personal boundaries, telling a child inappropriate sexual information.* | Can you think of some examples of psychological sexual abuse? This is more subtle and therefore often the hardest to recognize. It could be a parent looking to a daughter for emotional comfort that has a sexualized part to it. What are some other examples? |
| | *Examples include "inadvertent" inappropriate touching, household voyeurism, ridiculing a young girl's developing breasts, sexual hugs, or pornographic reading or video watching with a child.* | What are some examples of covert or more hidden or subtle abuse? |

TIME & TOPIC	FACILITATOR NOTES	DISCUSSION WITH WOMEN
	Examples include exhibitionism, fondling, French kissing, oral sex, or sexual penetration. (Adapted from *Helping Women Recover.* Copyright 1999 by S. Covington. This material is used by permission of John Wiley & Sons, Inc.)	What are some examples of more open or overt abuse? Here is a sample of a filled-out chart. **Sexual Abuse in Families** ————————————————▶ **Psychological Abuse** Sexual jokes Verbal harassment Violating boundaries Telling child inappropriate sexual information **Covert Abuse** Inappropriate touching Voyeurism Ridicule of body Sexual hugs Pornography **Overt Abuse** Exhibitionism French kissing Fondling Oral sex Penetration This is a lot to hear, so let's take a moment and do some self-soothing. Let's stand up and stretch, check in with ourselves, and breathe deeply before we move on.
18 min. **The little girl/child inside**	*Discuss.*	As we have been discussing families and our childhoods, it is important to realize that we all still have an inner child. You may be familiar with the term "inner child," but what does it mean? Our inner child, or that little girl inside of each of us, is that unique core self that we each possess who is the essence of our true self. The inner child is that part that is most natural, creative, playful, and innocent. It can also be a place where we hold on to childhood trauma and scars. It is when we let go of the external expectations and go within to reclaim our neglected inner child that we can deal most effectively with the outer world.

TIME & TOPIC	FACILITATOR NOTES	DISCUSSION WITH WOMEN
Exercise: *Getting to Know My Inner Child*		We are going to do a guided imagery called "Getting to Know My Inner Child."
		For this exercise, you can close your eyes or focus on the photographs you brought. Think about your childhood and pick an age between one and ten years old.
	Slowly ask the following questions, pausing between each one and leaving time for women to think about their responses.	Visualize the place where you lived: What was your room like? What was the color of the floor or the walls? Did you have a nickname? Did you have any pets? What were your favorite foods? Who were your best friends? What did you like to do with your best friends? What scared you? Did you have any secrets? What made you laugh? What did you want to do when you grew up? What does that child need from you now? Gently say good-bye to your inner child. Slowly open your eyes.
	Discuss.	Does anyone want to share anything about their "inner child"—the child that they found in the exercise?
		Sometimes it is helpful to "reparent" your inner child. The single most powerful and effective way to step safely out of rigid childhood roles and heal the wounds of the past is to begin to reparent yourself. No parent is perfect. But you can be a "good enough" parent and provide goodwill, support, understanding, warmth, and gentle caring to your inner child.
		To do this you need to understand and be attuned to your inner child's feelings and needs, and to commit to the reparenting (as you would an adoption). Attunement to your inner child can be a first step toward love and healing.
		The first steps on the reparenting path include being empathic, understanding, and

TIME & TOPIC	FACILITATOR NOTES	DISCUSSION WITH WOMEN
		gentle—validating the child's feelings and addressing them openly. After all, that is what a kind parent would do with a child. Listen carefully to what the inner child says, and then move to calmly reassure and soothe her. Others may feel comfortable reaching out to a close friend or partner, with whom they can be open and vulnerable, to allow this inner child to be held, loved, and nurtured by a trusted, intimate other.
	Say the following slowly.	Close your eyes again and picture your inner child one more time. Do you have a sense of your child's age? Feelings? Usual state of mind? Needs? Wants? Slowly open your eyes. . . . Look in your workbook and list all the clues you have about your inner child. You cannot treat a three-year-old like you would an eight-year-old. Even though it may be hard to look into yourself and face your inner child, reparenting your inner child is a critical part of self-healing that will allow you to know and love yourself and have healthy, intimate relationships in the future. Whenever you neglect your inner child, it interferes not only with your love relationships, but also with relationships in your wider support system, such as friendships.
		Without meeting the needs of your inner child, it can be difficult to meet your adult needs and the needs of those around you. Like any child, your inner child will continue to protest loudly until her needs are met. It is important to take the time to give yourself/your inner child the attention that she did not receive in childhood.

TIME & TOPIC	FACILITATOR NOTES	DISCUSSION WITH WOMEN
10 min. **Reflection and Homework**		Was there one thing that was particularly important for you today? We have been talking about families and our inner child. For your homework, look on pages 48 and 49 in your workbook. They are based on the visualization that you just did. The first activity asks you to describe your inner child. The second is a reparenting worksheet. The instructions are at the top of the page. For the inner child activity: Think about your childhood and describe it based on your visualization. In the space provided in the workbook, list all the clues and descriptions you have about your inner child. On the reparenting worksheet: Draw or describe how you would "reparent" your inner child. Devise a reparenting plan that suits your inner child's age and her needs. Try to meet one of your inner child's needs this week.

Session Notes

MODULE C: SESSION 8

Mind and Body Connection

■ Time

1 hour 30 minutes

■ Session Goal

Women will understand the connection between their mind and body.

■ Participant Learning Objectives

1. To understand emotional wellness

2. To learn to recognize feelings in the body

3. To learn how to express and contain feelings

4. To learn how to communicate more effectively

■ Session Overview

- The Mind-Body Connection
- Emotional Wellness
- *Exercise: Feelings and the Body*
- *Exercise: Communication and Feelings*
- *Reflection and Homework*

■ Materials and Equipment Needed

- Easel pad, felt pens, masking tape, crayons or colored pencils
- Participant's workbook
- Cassette or CD player and relaxing music
- Tissues
- Large sheets of butcher paper *(optional)*

Mind and Body Connection

TIME & TOPIC	FACILITATOR NOTES	DISCUSSION WITH WOMEN
2 min. **Quiet time**		Let us just sit quietly for a few minutes to let ourselves unwind, relax, and turn our attention to where we are now.
10 min. **Check-in**	*Discuss.*	How did you meet your inner child's needs (i.e., through reparenting) since our last session?
Goal for the session		Today we will be exploring the connection between the mind and the body.
33 min. **The mind-body connection**		We know that traumatic events can impact us in a variety of ways. One way is that our brains become overwhelmed, and it is difficult to make sense of or process what is happening. When this happens, individuals may fail to identify, understand, and process the traumatic event. These unprocessed, emotionally charged bits of trauma can be stored in our memory and in our bodies. Because these bits of trauma remain un-processed and unexpressed, women become vulnerable to being triggered. Therefore, things that happen today may trigger an emotional or physical response that almost seems as fresh as if the trauma were happen-ing today. For many women, the emotions they struggle with today are emotional reenactments of past abuse or trauma. As we discussed earlier, trauma can result in a disconnection between memory and

Duplicating this page is illegal. Do not copy this material without written permission from the publisher.

167

TIME & TOPIC	FACILITATOR NOTES	DISCUSSION WITH WOMEN
		feeling. Some women have memories without feeling and some have feelings without memory. One of the most important parts of healing is getting the feelings and the memories connected and expressed. This is part of the mind-body connection. When the feelings from the traumatic event are not expressed, they are often stored and then later expressed through the body. For example, difficult menstrual periods, eating disorders, headaches, chronic fatigue, thyroid disorders, back pain, and immune system suppression are some of the ways the body can express painful experiences. Clearly, our bodies and minds are very connected.
	Discuss.	What kinds of experiences have left you feeling numb?
	Discuss.	What role have alcohol and other drugs played in disconnecting you from your feelings?
	Discuss.	What has helped you reconnect with your feelings?
Emotional wellness		Trauma can profoundly impact a woman's emotional development. Addiction also impacts emotional development. A woman may be unaccustomed to having feelings. She may have shut down emotionally after a traumatic experience ("psychic numbing"), and she may need help finding the words to name how she feels. She may also need to learn both appropriate expression and containment. By *containment,* I mean having the ability to hold or contain a feeling until she wants to express it. Other women may be overwhelmed and flooded by feelings, and they need to learn expression and containment, too. When a woman learns expression

TIME & TOPIC	FACILITATOR NOTES	DISCUSSION WITH WOMEN
		and containment, she is no longer controlled by her feelings. She has now learned techniques to contain her feelings until she is in a safe or appropriate environment to express them. Earlier we discussed the zipper as a way of thinking about boundaries. The zipper is also useful when we think about containment. If you are flooded or overwhelmed by feelings, try to visualize having a zipper that allows you to close up your feelings and contain them. You can unzip the zipper when you want to express your feelings. In your workbook you will find Five Steps to Emotional Wellness on the top of page 52. Take a look at the five steps listed that can help us begin to create emotional wellness. 1. Become aware of when and how you are feeling. Tune in to yourself. 2. Try to locate the feeling in your body. Where are you experiencing the sensations? 3. Name the feeling—label it. 4. Express the feeling. 5. Learn to contain the feeling.
Exercise: *Feelings and the Body*	*The women may draw or trace their life-size body shape on butcher paper instead of using the workbook, if they prefer. Remember, some women may not want to close their eyes.*	Now, let us turn our attention to the bottom of page 52 in your workbook, to Feelings and the Body, where we can begin to work on items 1 and 2 on the emotional wellness list. Begin by closing your eyes. Think about your body and begin to notice what you are feeling and see if you can sense where it is in your body. Also notice how your face feels (the sensations you have in your face) when you have a feeling.

TIME & TOPIC	FACILITATOR NOTES	DISCUSSION WITH WOMEN
		Using colored pencils or crayons, show on the diagram where these feelings are located in your body. Also draw your facial expression. If you are having difficulty, be patient with yourself. This is hard to do, but it will get easier with practice.

Now let's do the exercise a little differently. Please go to page 53, Examples of Feelings. Pick a feeling from the list that you have felt in the past week or pick a feeling you have often.

Use a different colored pencil or crayon to show on the diagram where this feeling was located in your body. For instance, if you got mad or angry, perhaps your heart raced, your face turned red, or you began to sweat.

How did you express that feeling? Was it appropriate for the situation, the environment/surroundings, the intensity, the people involved? Did you regret expressing the feeling at that time?

How did you contain those feelings, or did you? How did your self-soothing techniques work in that situation? How might you handle your feelings and emotions differently now?

Here are some tips if you are feeling overwhelmed by a feeling. You will find these tips on page 53 of the workbook. They are there for you when you need them. Slow down or even stop what you are doing. Ask yourself, "What am I feeling?" Try to name the feeling. Ask yourself, "Does the intensity of this feeling match the situation?" Give yourself some time to sort this out. Then ask, "As I have this feeling, how old am I?" It is possible that your "inner child" may be |

TIME & TOPIC	FACILITATOR NOTES	DISCUSSION WITH WOMEN
		having this feeling. If the intensity does not match the current situation, or if you feel younger than your current age, the feeling is probably connected to the past.
35 min. **Exercise:** *Communication and Feelings*	*This depends on the size of the group—if the group is small, everyone can do this together.* *Need one timekeeper if you only have one group.* *After one minute, discuss.*	Another aspect of emotional wellness is how we communicate our feelings. The following exercise will help us develop our communication skills. I would like you to get into groups of three or four people. There are communication patterns that limit us or constrict us emotionally. These are often learned in families, or this emotional constriction can happen through abuse and trauma. First, we will experience forms of communication that do not connect people. Let us begin by having each group select a time-keeper. Now we will start the exercise by looking at each other for one minute but not speaking. You will notice that when you do not speak, you start to assume things about other people. You rely on other cues to tell you about that person's mood, thoughts, and so on. In dysfunctional or abusive families, this is often how people communicate. Kids learn to "read" or "assume" or "guess" what is going on because people do not communicate directly and openly. So relying on nonverbal communication without checking out assumptions creates miscommunication and disconnection between people.

TIME & TOPIC	FACILITATOR NOTES	DISCUSSION WITH WOMEN
		The next part of the exercise is about non-risky facts. Some families often talk only about safe or "nonrisky" facts.
	The facilitator shares first. Give an example from your own life: "I have two cats;" "I took the bus here."	I want you to share two nonrisky facts (different facts than the ones I used) with the people in your group. You will have about thirty seconds. Timekeepers, please track the time for each person.
		Nonrisky facts are another form of communication that limits people's connection to each other. In many families, another form of communication is opinions.
	Discuss a personal opinion (for approx. 30 seconds), such as "Women who work can be good mothers."	In your group, have each person share one strong opinion. You will have about one minute each. Timekeepers will track time.
		Opinions are important, but they need to be communicated as opinions rather than facts so they do not shut others out of the conversation. Sometimes strong, opinionated statements can hinder communication.
		"Poor me, ain't it awful?" stories are another form of communication.
	Give a personal example, such as "Nothing goes right for me. My new boss is so unhelpful, no wonder no one likes me at work."	In your group, share a "poor me" story. You will have about one minute each.
		Now we have experienced several forms of communication: nonverbal, nonrisky facts, opinions, and "poor me" stories.
		We can see how these forms of communication can limit or constrict a person's ability to connect with another. Let us shift to the

TIME & TOPIC	FACILITATOR NOTES	DISCUSSION WITH WOMEN
		language of feelings. Let us see how this compares. Many noncommunicative, dysfunctional families do not share feelings. It does not feel safe to do so. When children grow up in families that only communicate nonverbally, use nonrisky facts, give opinions as facts, and tell "poor me" stories, it is difficult to develop emotional wellness. So, we are going to learn about communicating feelings. Let us start out with the feeling of sadness.
	Again, you share first. *Share a sad feeling you might have, such as sadness around a recent death in the family or a sick friend.*	In your group, share something that has some sadness for you. You will have about one minute each. Remember, timekeepers, to keep time for each member.
	Share an angry feeling you might have, such as getting mad when your teenage son dropped out of school.	Now, let's talk about anger. In your group, share something that makes you angry. You will have one minute each.
	Share a feeling of joy, such as getting to see your first grandchild.	Now, let's talk about joy. In your group, share something that gives you a joyful feeling.
	Interrupt the groups after about thirty seconds and say, "Stop." Ask them how it feels to be interrupted. You will find the groups are irritated because they did not have time to talk and share their feelings. That is the point. Discuss how they felt when they were halted from sharing feelings, especially now that they are more bonded with their group,	

TIME & TOPIC	FACILITATOR NOTES	DISCUSSION WITH WOMEN
	having shared some personal feelings previously. What is happening between them is now more important than what the facilitator is saying or doing. After this discussion, give the groups time to finish sharing their joyful feelings.	How did it feel to share feelings with the group? For those of us who do not do this often, it may feel overwhelming. As you do this more and more, it will feel more comfortable. The sharing of feelings is an important part of the healing journey. This is why it is so important to have safe, supportive people in your life.
10 min. **Reflection and Homework**		Earlier, we talked about containment as a part of emotional wellness. Remember, emotional wellness is when you have a feeling, you can name it, you can locate it in your body, and you know how to express it. But if you choose not to express it at this time, and you hold it or contain it until there is a better time, that's "containment." Remember you can use a "zipper" to contain your feelings. This is different from "numbing" or "stuffing." For example, what if I came to work angry? Being angry all day at work or being angry in the group would not be appropriate. I have to save my feelings to process and deal with later. For your homework, as you go through your week, or in between now and the next session, continue to use your body chart, indicating where you are sensing feelings in your body. Also, write about one experience with containment.

The World of Feelings

■ **Time**

1 hour 30 minutes

■ **Session Goal**

Women will experience their feelings.

■ **Participant Learning Objectives**

1. To learn to recognize feelings
2. To learn to share feelings
3. To learn what empathy and compassion mean

■ **Session Overview**

• Feelings
• *Exercise: The Observer Self*
• Powerful, Shared Feelings
• *Exercise: Losses*
• Empathy
• *Exercise: Meeting a Feeling*
• *Reflection and Homework*

■ **Materials and Equipment Needed**

• Easel pad, felt pens, masking tape, crayons or colored pencils
• Cassette or CD player and relaxing music
• Tissues
• Participant's workbook

The World of Feelings

TIME & TOPIC	FACILITATOR NOTES	DISCUSSION WITH WOMEN
2 min. **Quiet time**		Let us just sit quietly for a few minutes to let ourselves unwind, relax, and turn our attention to where we are now.
10 min. **Check-in**		Identify where you are holding a feeling right now. Would anyone like to share an experience of containing a feeling from your homework assignment?
Goal for the session		Today we will continue to explore our feelings.
33 min. **Feelings**		In our last session, we began to talk about how we can develop emotional wellness. We did a communication exercise and also discussed containment. Expression and containment of feelings are both very important skills to learn. It is essential to remember that these are skills that we can learn only with time and practice. Expression and containment can be difficult when emotions arise immediately. It may feel strange, initially, to stop and work through the steps that help you contain and express your emotions appropriately, but it will eventually feel more comfortable. Some people believe that there are six basic, universal human emotions—anger, sadness, fear, happiness, disgust, and surprise. And then there are lots of other feelings that are secondary—such as guilt, pride, jealousy,

Duplicating this page is illegal. Do not copy this material without written permission from the publisher.

177

TIME & TOPIC	FACILITATOR NOTES	DISCUSSION WITH WOMEN
		and excitement. Expression and containment of feelings might seem simple at first, since there are so few basic emotions. What could be so difficult or complicated about identifying these feelings within us and expressing them to others? This is actually one of the most complicated tasks for many people—especially trauma survivors and recovering alcoholics and addicts. Women may experience many feelings that they feel they cannot share with others—or, at the other end of the continuum, they may feel "flooded" by feelings that cannot be contained. As we continue to talk about specific feelings, I'd like to share with you the concept of the Observer Self. This is a part of us that can help with containment. Many of us become overly reactive—we respond quickly and abruptly to other people's words and actions. The observer part of our self is that part that is capable of seeing reality without judging. It is the part that is a witness, not a judge. With practice, we can develop this part of ourselves.
Exercise: *The Observer Self*	*Read the following exercise slowly.*	Pick a situation you have been in recently where there was a problem and you experienced a lot of feelings. Now close your eyes and get totally involved in the scene of the problem. Keep focused on this situation. Be aware of how you are feeling as you involve yourself in this situation. . . . Notice the look on your face. . . . Notice the faces of others around you. . . . Notice how you move your body. . . . Notice the energy around you. . . . Just feel this experience for a moment as though it is happening right now. *(Pause.)*

TIME & TOPIC	FACILITATOR NOTES	DISCUSSION WITH WOMEN
		Now, leave the situation and move to a spot above it. . . . Look down on the scene you have just left behind and see it in its entirety. . . . Notice what you are doing. . . . Notice how others are reacting to you. . . . Look at the roles you and others are playing out. . . . Look at the place this is happening. . . . The city, the community, the culture you live in.
	Wait a few seconds.	Now, very slowly go back into the scene again. Totally immerse yourself back into the center of it. *(Allow a few seconds of silence.)* Be aware of how your body feels.
	Wait a few seconds.	Allow this scene to come to an end in whatever way you wish to resolve it for now.
		Gently, open your eyes and come back into this room.
	Discuss.	How did it feel to be totally in the situation?
	Discuss.	How did it feel to be observing it?
	Discuss.	Did you notice the difference in your body between being in the situation and being out of it? Explain.
		Most women will feel better when using the Observer Self. Learning and practicing the Observer Self will help in developing containment as well as learning more about ourselves.
		This is also a way to practice detachment. Detachment allows us to be less reactive. This is different from dissociation. With dissociation, you are disconnected and lost or split off from what is happening—removed from reality. With the Observer Self—or detachment—you are very present, developing and using more awareness and consciousness, not less. The Observer Self is a part of our strength, and using it empowers us.

TIME & TOPIC	FACILITATOR NOTES	DISCUSSION WITH WOMEN
Powerful, shared feelings		There are many feelings that women who have been abused share. Some of them are anger, loss, and shame.
		Anger—Sometimes women are angry at their abusers or at a person who they feel did not protect them (in some cases, their mothers). Sometimes they turn their anger inward, if they cannot express it, and become depressed. Some anger may come out in self-harming behavior (cutting or burning). And in some cases, anger is covering up another feeling, like fear. Fear or sadness can be underneath anger.
	Write anger *on the easel pad and list women's responses to the question. Common responses: yell, cry, hit their children, take time alone, exercise, throw things. Discuss.*	What are some of the ways women express anger?
	Write loss *on the easel pad and list women's experience of loss.*	Loss—Loss and grief are common experiences for women who have been abused and also for women with substance abuse problems. Some women have had multiple losses—of their children, their family members, their childhood innocence, or their health. Think back on your life and the losses you have experienced.
	Discuss grief. Typical responses: cry, isolate, pray, use rituals, make scrapbooks, write, honor anniversaries.	What is grief? (Grief is a response to loss; it includes sadness.) What are some ways that people grieve their losses?
		Shame—Many women experience shame. When women are abused either as children or as adults, they often feel ashamed and believe somehow it was their fault. Substance-abusing women often feel shame because of the stigma society places on addicted women.

TIME & TOPIC	FACILITATOR NOTES	DISCUSSION WITH WOMEN
	Write shame *on the easel pad and list women's responses to the question: Where does shame come from? Discuss.* *Shame is learned. It can come from cultural and social messages as well as from families.*	*Shame* is when a woman feels there is something wrong or bad about her. *Guilt* is when she feels there is something wrong or bad about her behavior. Shame can become a very destructive core issue. This is a deep-seated feeling, the roots of which can be difficult to unearth. Where does shame come from?
35 min. **Exercise:** *Losses*	*After two to three minutes, ask the question on the right.* *Give everyone an opportunity to briefly share.* *After the women have each shared a loss, ask them how they felt listening to the losses of others in the group. If women express sorrow or sadness for others' life experiences, label it "empathy."*	If you turn to page 59 in your workbook, you will find an exercise about losses in your life. Take a moment to write down some of your thoughts about losses in your life. Would everyone feel comfortable sharing one loss that they have had in their life?
Empathy		*Empathy* is the ability to share in another's feelings and emotions. Some of us seem to have empathy naturally, and others do not. Yet it is an important feeling to have in our relationships with others and for our own well-being. If a woman falls down and is frightened, you will probably sense her emotional distress. Likewise, in this group, we have had the

TIME & TOPIC	FACILITATOR NOTES	DISCUSSION WITH WOMEN
		opportunity to share feelings and empathize with each other. This has occurred through a process of sharing personal or intimate experiences, being nonjudgmental listeners for one another, and recognizing the same feelings in us that other group members feel. Developing the feeling of empathy enables us to be more compassionate. This is when we sense the suffering or trouble of another person, and we want to help. It is important for our relationships to learn to feel empathy and compassion. It is also important for us to feel compassion for ourselves and the pain we have suffered.
Exercise: _Meeting a Feeling_	_If this group has a great deal of difficulty with anger, then you may want to have all of the women choose anger as the feeling to understand better._ _When counting, keep your voice even, allowing the same amount of time between each number._	Pick a feeling that you have often, or one that you have had very recently, or one you would like to understand better. Close your eyes and begin to relax, noticing your breath as you breathe in and out. Begin to balance the breath by counting to four—breathe in to the count of four and out to the count of four. Notice any tension or pain anywhere in your body and gradually breathe your breath into these tense parts, breathing out the tension. . . . Feel yourself letting go. . . . Now, in your imagination, see yourself standing at the top of a staircase looking down at seven steps. You are going to descend to the bottom, knowing that there you will be completely relaxed and knowing that you can stop at any step. Now you are going down: one . . . two . . . three . . . four . . . five . . . six . . . seven.

TIME & TOPIC	FACILITATOR NOTES	DISCUSSION WITH WOMEN
		Now you are at the bottom, and you see yourself standing there with a light in your hand. This is the light of consciousness. You are going to go into your inner self. In your right hand is a lantern, shining a clear, bright light. And in your left hand is a cord that you can pull anytime you wish to be lifted up out of your inner self. You are safe and protected, and everything is fine. Now you are going to begin exploring your inner self. . . . Walk around and look for the feeling of _____. . . . And when you find the feeling, shine your light on it. See what it looks like. . . . Walk around it—look at its shape, size, and color. . . . Now ask your feeling what it is doing for you. . . . Then ask what it needs from you. . . . Ask the feeling if it has any more information for you. . . . Then thank the feeling for making itself known to you. . . . Shine the light on it, say good-bye, and explain that you may visit again. . . . Surround the feeling with love and appreciation.
	Pause. *Allow about three to five minutes for women to draw their feeling.*	Now go back to the bottom of the stairs and begin to walk up the seven stairs to the top . . . seven . . . six . . . five . . . four . . . three . . . two . . . one. Then walk outside the house. . . . Begin to bring yourself back into this room by noticing your feet on the floor. . . . Slowly open your eyes. Now, turn to page 62 in your workbook so you can draw a picture of the feeling you met—it may be a specific shape, design, or symbol. Share your drawing and tell us what you learned from the feeling—what it does for you, what it needs, and so on.

TIME & TOPIC	FACILITATOR NOTES	DISCUSSION WITH WOMEN
10 min. **Reflection and Homework**		What was an important part of today's group for you? Practice your Observer Self in two situations before our next meeting. Also, notice when you feel empathy for another or compassion for yourself.

Session Notes

Healthy Relationships: Wheel of Love

■ **Time**

1 hour 30 minutes

■ **Session Goal**

Women will learn the elements of a healthy relationship.

■ **Participant Learning Objectives**

1. To be able to define what a healthy relationship is

2. To understand how respect, mutuality, and compassion are at the core of a loving relationship

■ **Session Overview**

- Defining a Healthy Relationship

- Creating a Healthy Relationship

- The Wheels: The Relationship Wheel and the Power and Control Wheel

- *Exercise: The Relationship Wheel*

- Wheel of Love

- *Exercise: Love Collage*

- *Reflection and Homework*

■ **Materials and Equipment Needed**

- Easel pad, felt pens, masking tape

- Participant's workbook

- Cassette or CD player and relaxing music

- VCR and monitor

- Magazines for collage exercise

- A piece of poster board for each participant

- Glue sticks and scissors for group to share

- Tissues

- *Beyond Trauma* client video

Healthy Relationships: Wheel of Love

TIME & TOPIC	FACILITATOR NOTES	DISCUSSION WITH WOMEN
2 min. **Quiet time**		Let us just sit quietly for a few minutes to let ourselves unwind, relax, and turn our attention to where we are now.
10 min. **Check-in**		When and how did you use the Observer Self we learned about in the last session? What was the result? Describe a situation where you felt empathy or compassion.
Goal for the session		In today's session, we will learn about the elements of a healthy relationship.
25 min. **Defining a healthy relationship**	*Discuss and write responses on the easel pad.* *Discuss.* *Discuss and write responses on the easel pad.*	What is a healthy relationship? Have you had one or seen one? What did it look like? A healthy relationship is one where each person • *feels a greater sense of zest, vitality, and energy.* For example, you spend time with a friend, and when you part, you feel energized and alive. This happens because you are both putting energy into the relationship—and the energy is moving between you. Several days later you meet a friend, and afterward you feel depleted and exhausted. This may have happened because you were giving (providing energy to the relationship), and your friend was just taking.

TIME & TOPIC	FACILITATOR NOTES	DISCUSSION WITH WOMEN
	Discuss. (Covington and Dosher 2000.)	• *feels more able to act and does act.* A healthy relationship empowers you to act, and you feel free to take action in your life. • *has a more accurate perception of herself and the other person.* Because I am in this relationship with you, I see parts of myself that I would not see or know if I were alone. • *feels a greater sense of self-worth.* I feel good about myself in this relationship with you. • *feels more connected to the other person and feels a greater motivation for connections with other people beyond those in this specific relationship.* As time goes on, I feel more and more connected to you, and I also feel a desire to have friends and be connected to others (Miller 1986, 1990). Let us take a look at page 66 in the workbook, the Relationship Wheel. The core of healthy relationships is respect, mutuality, and compassion. **Relationship Wheel**

TIME & TOPIC	FACILITATOR NOTES	DISCUSSION WITH WOMEN
		Respect *Respect* is the appreciation of someone's values, and it begins to happen when we see that person's integrity. We often earn respect when we are willing to do the "right thing" or take the "right action," particularly when the choice is difficult. **Mutuality** *Mutuality* means there is an equal investment in the relationship. Each person has a willingness and desire to see the other as well as be seen, to hear the other as well as be heard, and to respect the other's vulnerability as well as be vulnerable. Mutuality also means that there is an awareness of the "we," not a sole focus on two "I's." **Compassion** *Compassion* is similar to empathy, but it occurs on a deeper level. *Empathy* is understanding others' feelings and being able to feel with them. *Compassion* means that we go a step further and join with them in their struggle or pain. When we are compassionate, we lend ourselves to another's process—we give of ourselves in order to be with the other emotionally.
Creating a healthy relationship		The following are some of the steps toward creating a healthy relationship: **Similarities** Similarities of temperament and shared interests between partners are certainly desirable, important, and fun. However, some of the more important similarities are the role of the relationship in each person's life and a shared vision of the future. Support for sobriety is also a crucial

TIME & TOPIC	FACILITATOR NOTES	DISCUSSION WITH WOMEN
		similarity if one of the partners is committed to recovery. **Ability to Deal with Change** Life is always changing, requiring us to change and adapt along with it. Because people do change, their needs and perspectives on life are also bound to change over time. In love relationships, the changing needs of one of the partners can cause a major relationship conflict. Therefore, the ability to deal effectively with change is a crucial skill in relationships. **Compatible Values** Some couples never discussed or paid attention to each other's values when they met. When a relationship moves into any kind of depth, values inevitably come into play. Discussing values, however, is not enough. People's *real* values are reflected in how they live and what they do, rather than just what they say. Learning about people's values by observation takes time. **Effective, Open Communication** Good communication is fundamental to all human relationships. The clarity of intent behind the message is one key to being understood. When a speaker is not aware of her or his motives or is not clear about her or his intent when speaking, and when words or body language don't fit the context, then the result is a mixed message. Good, clear communication can reduce conflict by eliminating needless misunderstandings or building of resentments. **Effective Conflict/Anger Resolution** The closer the love relationship, the more individual differences become evident—and the greater the possibility of conflict.

TIME & TOPIC	FACILITATOR NOTES	DISCUSSION WITH WOMEN
		Not only are differences to be expected, but they can be wonderful assets in a relationship. Differences may also become challenges, particularly if there is no open communication, and negotiation skills are lacking. Anger is not necessarily negative, as long as it is clear, is confined to an "I" statement that expresses an individual's feeling of frustration, and bears no threat of violence.
		Effective Negotiation
		Negotiation is at the heart of conflict resolution through problem solving. One way to think about negotiation is in terms of needs and wants. Needs are essential things that a person has to have; wants are preferences. In a relationship, one person's needs should have preference over the other person's wants. Another way to negotiate is to think about what the relationship needs versus what each individual may need or want.
		Firm Personal Boundaries
		People have physical, emotional, and intellectual boundaries that can be violated in different ways. In order to create a strong love relationship, it is important for each person not only to know when and how to set clear limits but also to accept and honor the boundaries and limits set by the partner. Ideally, personal boundaries are based on your own internal cues, not on a reaction to external triggers.
		Healthy Sexual Expression
		Healthy sexuality is a source of sensual and physical pleasure. It can be an expression of trust, of love, of tenderness, of fondness, of creativity, of playfulness. Sexuality is a powerful form of communication. It is important for partners to identify what

TIME & TOPIC	FACILITATOR NOTES	DISCUSSION WITH WOMEN
		they communicate or—more commonly— what they *don't* communicate to each other about sex. Building a climate of intimacy in which they feel free to express their sensuality and sexuality with each other is crucial.

Shared Quality Time

The issue of time is not a simple formula. In our demanding world, there can be vast differences between the time needs and the time availability of two partners. At its best, quality time is leisure time, open-ended, without built-in schedules or endings. It is time in which events, communication, and activities are allowed to unfold at their own pace, without a specific agenda. It requires nothing except a couple's willingness to be with each other openly, accepting and allowing whatever comes.

Friendship

Friendship is the cornerstone of intimate relationships. Friendship certainly is not a precondition for starting an intimate love relationship. And yet it is hard to imagine that over time a relationship could evolve into a healthy, successful, loving partnership without developing a strong element of friendship (Covington and Beckett 1988).

The steps to healthy relationships we have talked about are by no means limited to romantic-love partnerships. They are important for any relationship that holds the promise of openness and intimacy—including friendship. |

TIME & TOPIC	FACILITATOR NOTES	DISCUSSION WITH WOMEN
The wheels: The Relationship Wheel and the Power and Control Wheel		Now let us look again at the two "wheels": the Relationship Wheel and the Power and Control Wheel, which we discussed in an earlier session. They are on page 69 in your workbook.
		In the center of the Relationship Wheel are respect, mutuality, and compassion.
		Power and Control Wheel
	(Duluth Domestic Abuse Intervention Project, 202 E. Superior St., Duluth, MN 55802.)	
	Discuss.	The Power and Control Wheel shows power and control at the center of violence and abuse. Do you remember the beginning sessions, when we discussed power and control? What roles do power and control play in your current relationships?
		Earlier we also looked at various examples of abuse on the Power and Control Wheel shown on page 70 in your workbook.

TIME & TOPIC	FACILITATOR NOTES	DISCUSSION WITH WOMEN
		Power and Control Wheel 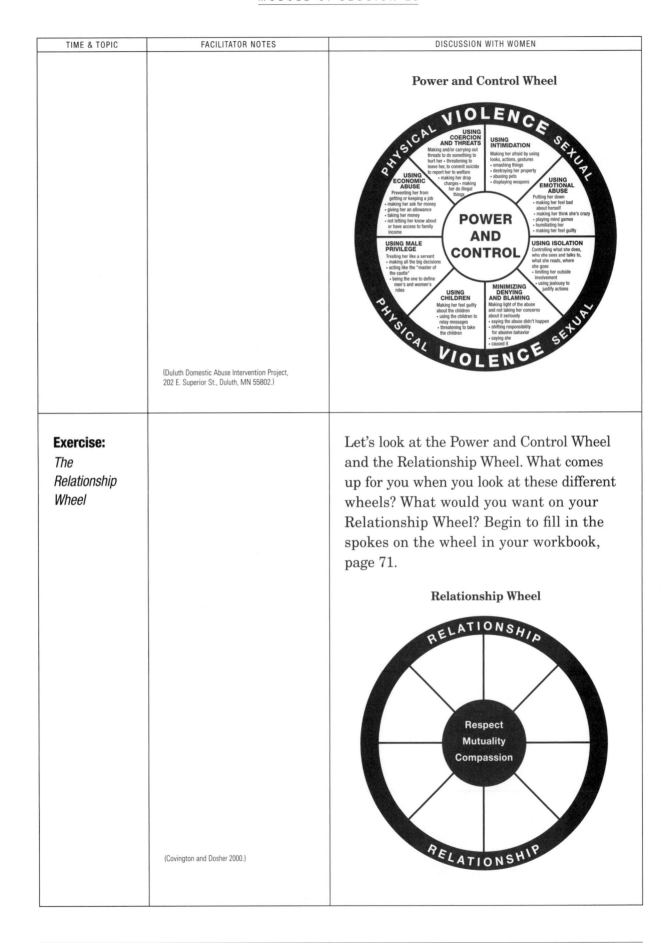
	(Duluth Domestic Abuse Intervention Project, 202 E. Superior St., Duluth, MN 55802.)	
Exercise: *The Relationship Wheel*		Let's look at the Power and Control Wheel and the Relationship Wheel. What comes up for you when you look at these different wheels? What would you want on your Relationship Wheel? Begin to fill in the spokes on the wheel in your workbook, page 71. **Relationship Wheel**
	(Covington and Dosher 2000.)	

TIME & TOPIC	FACILITATOR NOTES	DISCUSSION WITH WOMEN
Wheel of love	*Draw and then discuss the Wheel of Love on an easel pad.* (Covington and Dosher 2000.)	What is love? Love is created by respect, mutuality, and compassion. Love is both a feeling and a behavior. **Wheel of Love** **MUTUALITY RESPECT** **LOVE** **COMPASSION**
Video: *Beyond Trauma* Client video • CONCLUSION	*Show video: Segment 6.*	The video emphasizes the importance of supportive relationships in our lives. They help to sustain recovery and healing.
43 min. **Exercise:** *Love Collage*	*You will need to leave time at the end of the exercise for each woman to briefly share her collage.*	We are going to create a collage about love. We have many magazines that you can cut from as well as felt pens for you to draw with or enhance the magazine pictures. Each person will have her own poster board but will need to share glue and scissors with others in the group. I would like you to arrange images, pictures, or drawings into three sections in your collage: those that depict for you love in the past, love in the present, and love in the future (what you hope for in the future). You will have about twenty-five to thirty minutes.

TIME & TOPIC	FACILITATOR NOTES	DISCUSSION WITH WOMEN

10 min.
 	
Reflection and Homework
	Discuss
	
	At right, you will find a smaller version of the Relationship Scale that appears in the workbook.
	
	(Adapted from *Leaving the Enchanted Forest: The Path from Relationship Addiction to Intimacy* by Stephanie Covington and Liana Beckett. 1988. HarperCollins Publishers.)
		What was the most important part of the session today? What did you learn about yourself or your relationships?
		
		For your homework assignment, turn to page 73 in your workbook, where you will find a Relationship Scale.
		
		The Relationship Scale
		
		1. Similarities
		   1 2 3 4 5 6 7 8 9 10
		
		2. Ability to Deal with Change
		   1 2 3 4 5 6 7 8 9 10
		
		3. Compatible Values
		   1 2 3 4 5 6 7 8 9 10
		
		4. Effective, Open Communication
		   1 2 3 4 5 6 7 8 9 10
		
		5. Effective Conflict/Anger Resolution
		   1 2 3 4 5 6 7 8 9 10
		
		6. Effective Negotiation
		   1 2 3 4 5 6 7 8 9 10
		
		7. Firm Personal Boundaries
		   1 2 3 4 5 6 7 8 9 10
		
		8. Healthy Sexual Expression
		   1 2 3 4 5 6 7 8 9 10
		
		9. Shared Quality Time
		   1 2 3 4 5 6 7 8 9 10
		
		10. Friendship
		   1 2 3 4 5 6 7 8 9 10
		
		1. I would like you to think about one of your current relationships (it does not need to be sexual).

TIME & TOPIC	FACILITATOR NOTES	DISCUSSION WITH WOMEN
		2. Next, circle the number on the scale that shows where you rate your relationship now; your rating should be based on specific behaviors or situations. The number 1 represents the low end of the scale and 10 represents the high end. 3. Mark with an arrow the place on the scale where you want your relationship to be. 4. Finally, choose one item from the list that for you is a top priority. Think about what you can do to change this in your relationship, and consider discussing your wish with your partner. Continue to think about the love in your life. Keep working on your collage if you like— write a poem, draw a picture, write a song, use clay, use any creative means, but do something to express your feelings about the love you have and want in your life. You may also want to continue filling in the "spokes" of your Relationship Wheel with the things that are important to you in a relationship.
	As the facilitator, you may also want to bring an object to the next session.	Please bring something important to you to the next session. It may be an actual object (e.g., a special stone) or something that represents or symbolizes what is important to you (e.g., a photograph or drawing). Also, please bring your love collage to the group next time.

MODULE C: SESSION 11

Endings and Beginnings

▤ Time

1 hour 30 minutes

▤ Session Goal

Women will understand the importance of connection in their lives.

▤ Participant Learning Objectives

1. To learn how to end relationships respectfully

2. To recognize the important women in their lives

3. To understand the importance of connection and spirituality

▤ Session Overview

- Building an Altar

- Endings and Beginnings

- *Exercise: Appreciation*

- The Meaning and Importance of Spirituality

- Twelve Step Programs and Spirituality

- *Exercise: Meditation*

- *Exercise: Meaningful Women in Our Lives*

▤ Materials and Equipment Needed

- Pretty piece of fabric, scarf, or tablecloth

- Meaningful object *(optional)*

- Participant's workbook

- Easel pad, felt pens, masking tape

- Cassette or CD player and relaxing music

- Tissues

Endings and Beginnings

TIME & TOPIC	FACILITATOR NOTES	DISCUSSION WITH WOMEN
2 min. **Quiet time**		Let us just sit quietly for a few minutes to let ourselves unwind, relax, and turn our attention to where we are now.
Goal for the session		This is our time to say good-bye. Today we will talk about the connections we have formed in the group and in our lives outside of the group. We will discuss the importance and meaning of these connections in our past, present, and future lives.
40 min. **Building an altar (check-in)**	*Put a pretty piece of cloth, scarf, or tablecloth in the center of the group on the floor to "hold" the objects the women have brought. You may also want to share and place an object.* *Optional: As a group, you may also want to do something together that is meaningful, such as make a clay sculpture, sing a song, or write a poem.*	For those of you who brought objects, would you please share a little about what your item means to you and why you chose to share it with us today? When you finish sharing, please place your object in the center of the circle. You can also place posters, collages, poems, songs, and anything else you brought in the center, too. In some ways in this group, we have created an "altar"—a place where we have put things that are special to us in our lives. These things represent or symbolize what is important to us.

TIME & TOPIC	FACILITATOR NOTES	DISCUSSION WITH WOMEN
Endings and beginnings		This session is about endings and beginnings. We are at the end of our eleven sessions together. Over these past sessions, we have looked at trauma and abuse in women's lives; we have talked about how common it is in our lives; we have examined how it has impacted us; and we have learned some skills to help us heal. And now it is time to close our group.
	Discuss and write the following ideas on the easel pad.	When you think about ending a relationship, what things come to mind?
		How have you ended relationships in the past?
		Have you ended a relationship well?
		If so, how did you do it?
	Be sure these ideas are included: • *Be direct and honest.* • *Speak with "I" statements rather than "you" statements.* • *Express feelings being experienced in the present.* • *Assume personal responsibility for change.* • *Decide the level of physical and emotional intimacy you want with the person.* • *Act in a timely fashion— establish and adhere to agreed-upon timelines by which changes should occur.* • *Let the other person know what you appreciate about her or him.*	How do you end a relationship in a healthy, respectful way? These are some guidelines that may be helpful when ending a relationship.

TIME & TOPIC	FACILITATOR NOTES	DISCUSSION WITH WOMEN
	• *Let the other person know what you appreciated about the relationship.* • *Tell her or him what you wish you'd been able to do differently.* *Depending on the circumstances, this group may have the option of continuing together.*	I think there are a few points in this list that can be helpful to us today: 1. Be direct and honest. Throughout our group sessions, we have been learning how to be direct and honest with each other—as well as with ourselves. We have also learned that honesty without sensitivity can feel brutal. We are being direct, honest, and sensitive about our ending. 2. Decide the level of intimacy or contact you want with one another. Even though our group is ending, some of you may decide to continue seeing and supporting each other. 3. Act in a timely fashion. We were clear about the timeline of the group when we began. The starting and ending times of each session, as well as when the group would end, were discussed. Of course, this part of ending a relationship is easier when it is a group relationship, not a love relationship. But in ending any relationship, being clear about the timeline is important.

TIME & TOPIC	FACILITATOR NOTES	DISCUSSION WITH WOMEN
Exercise: *Appreciation*	*Allow each woman some time to express something that she appreciates about each woman in the group.* *Allow each woman some time to express something that she appreciates about the group.*	4. Express appreciation about the other. We are going to take some time for each of you to express something that you appreciate about each other. 5. Express appreciation about the relationship. You also have an opportunity to share something that you have appreciated about the group. Over the past ten sessions, we have learned that one of the essential parts of healing from trauma is moving out of isolation and learning to create connection. We have learned that sharing about ourselves and sharing our feelings with others helps to create connection. The amazing thing about deep connection is that it never really ends. When you have a deep connection with another, it stays with you—even if you do not have contact with the person, you often still carry her or him with you.
25 min. **The meaning and importance of spirituality**	*On the easel pad, write the word* religion *and make a list of what the word means for the group. Then write the group's responses to* what spirituality *means. If no one mentions connection, then add this to the spirituality list.* *Read the definition slowly, allowing the women to think about what it means to them.*	There are many ways to heal from trauma. Spirituality is one way to gain serenity and a sense of connection. Often, there is confusion about the terms *spirituality* and *religion*. Let us look at what religion means, and then at what spirituality means. One definition of *spirituality* is "oneness, wholeness, connection to the universe; belief in something greater than yourself; trust in a higher or deeper part of yourself."

TIME & TOPIC	FACILITATOR NOTES	DISCUSSION WITH WOMEN
		Connection is a word very commonly associated with the word *spirituality*. Spirituality often means connection on multiple levels: • connection with self • connection with others • connection with nature, the earth • connection to a Higher Power The metaphor of a garden, reflected in the following quote, is helpful in describing how women experience and express their spirituality. Gardens can be entered in a thousand ways and at any time. You can enter in childhood by the door of your home and continue to cultivate your garden through the whole of your life. Or the door can slam shut in adolescence, leaving you lost and searching for what T. S. Eliot called "the unknown, remembered gate." You can enter through a gate that is wide or narrow or so overgrown with ivy and weeds that you have to search carefully for the opening. . . . But who could argue that a garden of daisies and hollyhocks was more developed than a garden of artichokes and asparagus? Who could claim that a garden with a great variety of flowers was more inclusive and therefore more highly evolved than one that contained only roses? All gardens, of course, must be cultivated if they are to grow, but each one comes to maturity in its own time, in its own way. One of the ways that people develop their spirituality is through practice. Women in Twelve Step programs practice Steps that

(Reprinted with permission from *The Feminine Face of God: The Unfolding of the Sacred in Women* by Sherry Ruth Anderson and Patricia Hopkins. 1993. Bantam Books.)

TIME & TOPIC	FACILITATOR NOTES	DISCUSSION WITH WOMEN
	Discuss and write ideas on the easel pad.	are based on spiritual principles. With practice comes a deeper spiritual connection and healing. We know that trauma disconnects women from themselves, others, and the world around them. It also disconnects women from their spirituality. Can you think of some examples of how a woman can practice to get more in touch with her spiritual side? Examples include, but are not limited to • quiet time • prayer • meditation • centering activities such as singing or listening to music • being out in nature • keeping a journal • attending church, synagogue, mosque, temple • helping others in need • creating personal altars This might be a grouping of personal items that are meaningful to you, such as a seashell from a memorable walk on the beach after a month of sobriety, a collar from a beloved pet, a photo of a significant person or event, a pinecone from a hike, a family photo, a prize from a fair, a candle. It can be a special location where you can stop, pause, reflect, pray, meditate, and feel connected to a sense of time and place, history, accomplishment, and hope.

TIME & TOPIC	FACILITATOR NOTES	DISCUSSION WITH WOMEN
		• learning from others Holding a quiet, safe, respectful time where you, as women, can come together to share your hopes, dreams, and what is meaningful can be empowering. Sharing intimate stories can be inspiring and freeing.
		• celebrations! Integrate celebrations, rituals, and traditions into your daily routine. As women, we need to learn to celebrate ourselves, even when we are alone. One example is celebrating milestones: birthdays, receiving a high school diploma or GED, staying clean and sober, sticking with an exercise program, and facing a tough problem. It is important to celebrate internal and external accomplishments. These celebrations can offer stability, direction, connection to your cultural roots, and reinforcement of positive conceptions of womanhood. Spiritual activities and rituals offer relationship and connection (with family, community, and peers), beliefs and values, healing, protection, support (others committed to helping you reach your goals), and celebration (joy and hope).
	Discuss and encourage women to pursue activities that feed them spiritually.	How much time do you give yourself each week to allow for personal reflection, meditation, cultural traditions, or discussions about life, meaning, and values?
	Discuss.	If you want to change what you are doing now, how can you make that happen?

TIME & TOPIC	FACILITATOR NOTES	DISCUSSION WITH WOMEN
Twelve Step programs and spirituality		In a Twelve Step program, Step Eleven recommends prayer and meditation as the means of cultivating "conscious contact" with a Higher Power. This nurtures a spiritual awakening that opens a connection and helps the healing journey from trauma, as well as from addiction. Spiritual practices such as prayer and meditation are important to your spiritual life and help to form a relationship with yourself, others, your surroundings, and a Higher Power. Spirituality helps build a strong bridge of connection to many parts of a woman's life.
Exercise: *Meditation*		Meditation can help us find serenity in our world through solitude and stillness. It can help us feel calm and at peace deep inside. Let us take a few minutes to practice meditation. You can do this with your eyes open or closed.
		Breathing is central to meditation. I am going to guide you as you begin to focus on your breath. Please put both of your feet on the floor, empty your hands and laps, sit up straight, and close your eyes. If you prefer to keep your eyes open, focus on the item you brought in the center of our circle.
	Use a slow, calm voice.	Now, focus on the breath at the very end of your nose. Slowly count to four as you inhale. Then count to four as you exhale. Keep breathing and counting. Follow your breath—the air—as it flows in and out of your nose.
	Continue this for one to two minutes. Then be silent for thirty seconds.	If other thoughts come to mind, just let them pass on through. Come back and focus on your breath. Count to four as you inhale. Count to four as you exhale.

TIME & TOPIC	FACILITATOR NOTES	DISCUSSION WITH WOMEN
		If feelings come up, recognize them but then let them pass. Let them go. Just keep bringing your attention back to your breathing, deep breaths going slowly in and slowly out again.
		If you find your mind wandering, that is normal; do not be upset with yourself. Just bring your mind gently back and concentrate on your breathing.
	Be silent for about thirty seconds.	Please bring your attention back to the room. Feel your feet on the ground; feel your backs in your chairs. When you are ready, open your eyes.
	Wait for everyone to open their eyes and be attentive.	How did that feel?
	Debrief the exercise.	You can create the same kind of silent space for yourself by taking a few minutes to do this every day, maybe several times a day.
		Meditation can help calm and soothe us. Remember, meditation is a way to create connection with ourselves and our Higher Power.
		This is another skill we can use on our healing journey.
23 min. **Exercise:** *Meaningful Women in Our Lives*	*Have the women stand and hold hands in a circle around the objects in the center.*	And now it's time to begin our closing. We're going to do an exercise that will help us create and experience ongoing connection. Please come together in a circle. Let's close our eyes for a minute and think about the women who have been important to us— who have been meaningful in our lives. It may be your mother, your grandmother,

TIME & TOPIC	FACILITATOR NOTES	DISCUSSION WITH WOMEN
		another family member, a teacher, a therapist, or someone else. There may be one woman or there may be several. Think about what you have received from her, what you learned, or what qualities you respected.
		When you are ready to share, please open your eyes.
	Allow time for each woman to share.	Let us go around the circle having each of us say the name of the woman (or women) who have touched our lives and made a difference. Also, say one or two words about what you received from her, what you learned, or what qualities you respected.
	When the women have shared, close with these words.	What you each have been given is always there for you. . . . These enduring connections and their gifts are always there for you to receive. You just have to reach out and remember.
		And as we stand here, we have created a protective circle of women (both us and the special women in our lives) around the things that are important to each of us, and a protective circle of love. This is an important part of healing—having a protective circle.
		Our group has come to an end, but you can always carry this experience with you as you make new beginnings and decisions about the next steps in your life.
		With each ending, space is created for new beginnings. I wish you all a great new beginning on your healing journey!

PART FOUR

RESOURCES

Academy of Traumatology
1564 Keily Run
Tallahassee, FL 32301
(850) 656-7158
www.traumatologyacademy.org

Adult Children of Alcoholics World Service Organization, Inc.
ACA WSO
PO Box 3216
Torrance, CA 90510
(310) 534-1815
www.adultchildren.org

Alcoholics Anonymous
Grand Central Station
PO Box 459
New York, NY 10163
(212) 870-3400
www.aa.org

American Psychological Association
750 First Street NE
Washington, DC 20002-4242
(800) 374-2721
www.apa.org

Association of Traumatic Stress Specialists
ATSS
PO Box 2747
Georgetown, TX 78627
(512) 868-3677
www.atss-hq.com

Co-Dependents Anonymous (CoDA)

Fellowship Services Office (FSO)
PO Box 33577
Phoenix, AZ 85067-3577
(602) 277-7991
www.codependents.org

Emotions Anonymous International

PO Box 4245
St. Paul, MN 55104-0245
(651) 647-9712
www.emotionsanonymous.org

Family Violence Prevention Fund

383 Rhode Island Street, Suite #304
San Francisco, CA 94103-5133
(415) 252-8900
www.fvpf.org

The International Society for Traumatic Stress Studies

ISTSS
60 Revere Drive, Suite 500
Northbrook, IL 60062
(847) 480-9028
www.istss.org

Narcotics Anonymous

NAWS, Inc.
PO Box 9999
Van Nuys, CA 91409
(818) 773-9999
www.na.org

National Center for PTSD

(802) 296-6300
www.ncptsd.org

National Clearinghouse on Child Abuse and Neglect Information

Administration for Children and Families
330 C Street SW
Washington, DC 20447
(800) 394-3366
www.calib.com/nccanch

National Domestic Violence Hot Line
> PO Box 161810
> Austin, TX 78716
> (800) 799-SAFE (7233) or (800) 787-3224 (TTY)
> www.ndvh.org

National Mental Health Association
> 2001 N. Beauregard Street, 12th Floor
> Alexandria, VA 22311
> (800) 969-6642
> www.nmha.org

National Mental Health Consumers' Self-Help Clearinghouse
> 1211 Chestnut Street, Suite 1207
> Philadelphia, PA 19107
> (800) 553-4539
> www.mhselfhelp.org

Parents Anonymous
> 675 West Foothill Blvd., Suite 220
> Claremont, CA 91711-3475
> (909) 621-6184
> www.parentsanonymous.org

Posttraumatic Stress Disorder Alliance
> PTSD Alliance Resource Center
> (877) 507-PTSD (7873)
> www.ptsdalliance.org

SelfAbuse.com
> Self-harming behavior (information)
> www.selfabuse.com

Sidran Institute
> 200 E. Joppa Road, Suite 207
> Baltimore, MD 21286
> (410) 825-8888
> www.sidran.org/resources

Survivors of Incest Anonymous World Service Office, Inc.
> PO Box 190
> Benson, MD 21018-9998
> (410) 893-3322
> www.siawso.org

FEDERAL RESOURCES

Bureau of Justice Statistics (BJS)
(202) 307-0765
www.ojp.usdoj.gov/bjs/

**SAMHSA's National Clearinghouse for Alcohol and
Drug Information (NCADI)**
(800) 729-6686 or (800) 487-4889 (TDD)
www.ncadi.samhsa.gov

SAMHSA's National Mental Health Information Center
(800) 789-2647
www.mentalhealth.samhsa.gov

SAMHSA's Substance Abuse Treatment Facility Locator
(800) 662-HELP (4357)
www.findtreatment.samhsa.gov

U.S. Department of Justice Office on Violence against Women
www.ojp.usdoj.gov/vawo

FEDERAL PUBLICATIONS

Available from The National Clearinghouse on Alcohol and Drug Information (NCADI):

Helping Yourself Heal: A Recovering Woman's Guide to Coping with Childhood Abuse Issues. (2003). Publication No. (SMA) 03-3789. Rockville, Md.: Center for Substance Abuse Treatment, U.S. Department of Health and Human Services, Substance Abuse and Mental Health Services Administration (www.samhsa.gov).

Substance Abuse Treatment: Addressing the Specific Needs of Women. (In press as of October 2003.) Treatment Improvement Protocol (TIP) Series. Rockville, Md.: Center for Substance Abuse Treatment, U.S. Department of Health and Human Services.

Substance Abuse Treatment and Domestic Violence. (2002). Treatment Improvement Protocol (TIP) Series. Publication No. (SMA) 02-3627. Rockville, Md.: Center for Substance Abuse Treatment, U.S. Department of Health and Human Services.

Substance Abuse Treatment and Trauma. (In press as of October 2003.) Treatment Improvement Protocol (TIP) Series. Rockville, Md.: Center for Substance Abuse Treatment, U.S. Department of Health and Human Services.

Substance Abuse Treatment for Persons with Child Abuse and Neglect Issues. (2002). Treatment Improvement Protocol (TIP) Series. Publication No. (SMA) 02-3694. Rockville, Md.: Center for Substance Abuse Treatment, U.S. Department of Health and Human Services.

REFERENCES

Alcoholics Anonymous World Services. 1996. *Analysis of the 1996 AA membership survey.* New York: Alcoholics Anonymous World Services.

Alderman, T. 1997. *The scarred soul: Understanding and ending self-inflicted violence.* Oakland, CA: New Harbinger Publications.

Alderman, T., and K. Marshall. 1998. *Amongst ourselves: A self-help guide to living with dissociative identity disorder.* Oakland, Calif.: New Harbinger Publications.

Alexander, M. 1996. Women with co-occurring addictive and mental disorders: An emerging profile of vulnerability. *American Journal of Orthopsychiatry* 66 (1): 10.

American Medical Association. 1998. Protecting our children: Sexual abuse of children is common, and too often undetected. *Journal of the American Medical Association* 280 (December 2):1888. http://www.medem.com/search/article_display.cfm?path=%5C%5CTANQUER-AY%5CM_ContentItem&mstr=/M_ContentItem/ZZZ9MAZQJAC.html&soc=JAMA/Archives&srch_typ=NAV_SERCH (accessed 2 July 2003).

American Psychiatric Association. 1994. *Diagnostic and statistical manual of mental disorders DSM-IV.* 4th ed. Washington, D.C.: American Psychiatric Association.

———. 2000. *Diagnostic and statistical manual of mental disorders DSM-IV-TR (text revision).* 4th ed. Washington, D.C.: American Psychiatric Association.

American Psychological Association. 1996. *Violence and the family: Report of the American Psychological Association presidential task force on violence and the family.* Washington, DC: American Psychological Association.

Anderson, S., and P. Hopkins. 1993. *The feminine face of God: The unfolding of the sacred in women.* New York: Bantam.

Aries, E. 1976. Interaction patterns and themes of male, female, and mixed groups. *Small Group Behavior* 7 (1): 7–18.

Bepko, C., ed. 1991. *Feminism and addiction.* New York: Haworth Press.

Berenson, D. 1991. Powerlessness: Liberation or enslaving? Responding to the feminist critique of the Twelve Steps. In *Feminism and addiction,* edited by C. Bepko, 67–80. New York: Haworth Press.

Berry C. 2003. *When helping you is hurting me.* New York: Crossroads Publishing Company.

Bloom, B., B. Owen, and S. Covington. 2003. *Gender responsive strategies: Research, practice, and guiding principles for women offenders.* Washington, D.C.: National Institute of Corrections.

Bloom, S. 2000. The sanctuary model. *Therapeutic Communities* 21 (2): 67–91.

Blume, S. 1997. Women: Clinical aspects. In *Substance abuse: A comprehensive textbook,* edited by J. Lowinson, P. Ruiz, A. Milkman, and J. Langrod, 645–54. Baltimore, Md.: Williams and Wilkins.

Brown, P., and J. Wolfe. 1994. Substance abuse and posttraumatic stress disorder comorbidity. *Drug and Alcohol Dependence* 35: 51–9.

Bureau of Justice Statistics (BJS). 1998. *National crime victimization survey.* Washington, D.C.: U.S. Department of Justice.

———. 1999. *Prior abuse reported by inmates and probationers.* Washington, D.C.: U.S. Department of Justice.

———. 2000a. *Intimate partner violence.* Washington, D.C.: U.S. Department of Justice.

———. 2000b. *Sexual assault of young children as reported to law enforcement: Victim, incident, and offender characteristics.* Washington, D.C.: U.S. Department of Justice.

———. 2003. Intimate partner violence, 1993–2001. *Bureau of Justice Statistics Crime Data Brief,* NCJ197838 (February).

Cappell, C., and R. Heiner. 1990. The intergenerational transmission of family aggression. *Journal of Family Violence* 5 (2): 135–52.

Carlson, B. 1990. Adolescent observers of marital violence. *Journal of Family Violence* 5: 285–99.

Carmen, E. H. 1995. Inner city community mental health: The interplay of abuse and race in chronically mentally ill women. In *Mental health: Racism and sexism,* edited by C. V. Willie, P. P. Rieker, B. M. Kramer, and B. S. Brown, 217–36. Pittsburgh, Pa.: University of Pittsburgh Press.

Clarke, J., and C. Dawson. 1998. *Growing up again: Parenting ourselves, parenting our children.* Center City, Minn.: Hazelden.

Commonwealth Fund. 1997. *The Commonwealth Fund survey of the health of adolescent girls.* Publication #252 (November). New York: Commonwealth Fund.

Cottler, L., W. Compton, D. Mager, E. Spitznagel, and A. Janca. 1992. Post-traumatic stress disorder among substance users from the general population. *American Journal of Psychiatry* 149 (5): 664–70.

Cottler, L., P. Nishith, and W. Compton. 2001. Gender differences in risk factors for trauma exposure and post-traumatic stress disorder among inner-city drug abusers in and out of treatment. *Comprehensive Psychiatry* 42 (2): 111–17.

Covington, S. 1994. *A woman's way through the Twelve Steps.* Center City, Minn.: Hazelden.

———. 1998a. The relational theory of women's psychological development: Implications for the criminal justice system. In *Female offenders: Critical perspectives and effective intervention,* edited by R. Zaplin, 113–31. Gaithersburg, Md.: Aspen Press.

———. 1998b. Women in prison: Approaches in the treatment of our most invisible population. *Women and Therapy Journal* 21 (1): 141–55.

———. 1999. *Helping women recover: A program for treating addiction (with a special edition for the CJ system).* San Francisco: Jossey-Bass.

———. 2000. *Awakening your sexuality: A guide for recovering women.* Center City, Minn.: Hazelden.

———. 2002. Helping women recover: Creating gender-responsive treatment. In *Handbook of women's addiction treatment: Theory and practice,* edited by S. L. A. Straussner and S. Brown, 52–72. San Francisco: Jossey-Bass.

Covington, S., and L. Beckett. 1988. *Leaving the enchanted forest: The path from relationship addiction to intimacy.* San Francisco: HarperCollins Publishers.

Covington, S., and B. Bloom. 2003. Gendered justice: Women in the criminal justice system. In *Gendered justice: Addressing female offenders,* edited by B. Bloom, 3–23. Durham: N.C.: Carolina Academic Press. Paper presented at the 52nd Annual Meeting of the American Society of Criminology, San Francisco (November 2000).

Covington, S., and A. Dosher. 2000. The discipline of compassion. Unpublished manuscript.

Covington, S., and J. Kohen. 1984. Women, alcohol, and sexuality. *Advances in Alcohol and Substance Abuse* 4 (1): 41–56.

Covington, S., and J. Surrey. 1997. The relational model of women's psychological development: Implications for substance abuse. In *Gender and alcohol: Individual and social perspectives,* edited by S. Wilsnack and R. Wilsnack, 335–51. New Brunswick, N.J.: Rutgers University Press.

Cramer, M. 2000. Issues in the treatment of dual diagnosis: PTSD and substance abuse in women. Presentation to DATA of Rhode Island, Providence, R.I. (October).

Dallam, S. J. 1997. The identification and management of self-mutilating patients in primary care. *The Nurse Practitioner* 22 (5): 151–8.

Davidson, J. 1993. Issues in the diagnosis of post-traumatic stress disorder. In *American Psychiatric Press review of psychiatry,* edited by J. M. Oldham, M. B. Riba, and A. Tasman, 141–55. Washington, D.C.: American Psychiatric Press.

Donziger, S. R., ed. 1996. *The real war on crime: The report of the national Criminal Justice Commission.* New York: HarperPerennial.

Duerk, J. 1993. *Circle of stones.* Philadelphia, P.A.: Innisfree Press, Inc.

Duluth Abuse Intervention Project. 1999. *Power and control wheel.* Duluth, Minn.: Minnesota Program Development.

Federal Bureau of Investigation. 1999. *Crime in the United States: Uniform crime reports, 1998.* Washington, D.C.: U.S. Department of Justice.

Figley, C. 2002. Compassion fatigue: Psychotherapists' chronic lack of self care. *Journal of Clinical Psychology* 58 (11): 1433–41.

Figley, C., R. Giel, S. Borgo, S. Briggs, and M. Harotis-Fatouros. 1995. Prevention and treatment of community stress: How to be a mental health expert at the time of disaster. In *Extreme stress and communities: Impact and intervention,* edited by S. E. Hobfoll and M. W. de Vries. London: Kluwer Academic Publishers.

Finkelstein, N. 1996. Using the relational model as a context for treating pregnant and parenting chemically dependent women. In *Chemical dependency: Women at risk,* edited by B. Underhill and D. Finnegan, 23–44. New York: Harrington Park Press/Haworth Press.

Godleski, L. 1997. Tornado disasters and stress responses. *KMA Journal* 95:145–8.

Haigh, R. 1999. The quintessence of a therapeutic environment: Five universal qualities. In *Therapeutic communities: Past, present and future,* edited by P. Campling and R. Haigh, 246–57. London: Jessica Kingsley Publishers.

Harris, M., and Community Connections Trauma Work Group. 1998. *Trauma recovery and empowerment.* New York: Simon and Schuster.

Harris, M., and R. Fallot. 2001. *Using trauma theory to design services systems.* San Francisco: Jossey-Bass.

Harvey, M. 1996. An ecological view of psychological trauma and trauma recovery. *Journal of Traumatic Stress* 9: 3–23.

Herman, J. 1992. *Trauma and recovery.* New York: HarperCollins.

———. 1997. *Trauma and recovery.* Rev. ed. New York: HarperCollins.

Hopper, J. 1998. *Child abuse: Statistics, research, resources.* Boston: Boston University School of Medicine.

Institute of Medicine. 1990. *Broadening the base of treatment for alcohol problems.* Washington, D.C.: National Academy of Sciences.

Janes, J. 1994. Their own worst enemy? Management and prevention of self-harm. *Professional Nurse* 9 (12): 838–41.

Kasl, C. 1992. *Many roads, one journey.* New York: HarperCollins.

Kessler, R., A. Sonnega, E. Bromet, M. Hughes, C. Nelson, and N. Breslau. 1999. Epidemiological risk factors for trauma and PTSD. In *Risk factors for PTSD,* edited by R. Yehuda. Washington, D.C.: American Psychiatric Press.

Kilpatrick, D., R. Acierno, B. Saunders, H. Resnick, C. Best, and P. Schnurr. 1998. *National survey of adolescents: Executive summary.* Charleston, S.C.: Medical University of South Carolina, National Crime Victims Research and Treatment Center.

Kilpatrick, D., and B. Saunders. 1997. *Prevalence and consequences of child victimization: Results from the national survey of adolescents, final report.* Washington, D.C.: Office of Justice Programs, National Institute of Justice.

Levine, P. 1997. *Waking the tiger: Healing trauma.* Berkeley, Calif.: North Atlantic Books.

Linehan, M. 1993. *Skills training manual for treating borderline personality disorder.* New York: Guilford Press.

Lorde, A. 1984. *Sister outsider.* Freedom, Calif.: Crossing Press.

McWilliams, N., and J. Stein. 1987. Women's groups led by women: The management of devaluing transferences. *International Journal of Group Psychotherapy* 37 (2): 139–62.

Messina, N., W. Burdon, and M. Prendergast. 2001. *A profile of women in prison based therapeutic communities.* Draft. Los Angeles: UCLA Integrated Substance Abuse Program, Drug Abuse Center.

Miller, D. 1991. Are we keeping up with Oprah: A treatment and training model for addiction and interpersonal violence. In *Feminism and addiction,* edited by C. Bepko, 103–26. New York: Haworth Press.

Miller, D., and L. Guidry. 2001. *Addictions and trauma recovery: Healing the body, mind, and spirit.* New York: W. W. Norton & Co.

Miller, J. 1982. *Women and power.* Work in Progress Working Paper Series, no. 82-01. Wellesley, Mass.: Stone Center, Wellesley College.

———. 1986. *What do we mean by relationships?* Work in Progress Working Paper Series, no. 22. Wellesley, Mass.: Stone Center, Wellesley College.

———. 1990. *Connections, disconnections, and violations.* Work in Progress Working Paper Series, no. 33. Wellesley, Mass.: Stone Center, Wellesley College.

Minkoff, K. 1989. An integrated treatment model for dual diagnosis of psychosis and addiction. *Hospital and Community Psychiatry* 40 (10): 1031–6.

Mirowsky, J., and C. Ross. 1995. Sex differences in distress: Real or artifact? *American Sociological Review* 60 (3): 449–68.

Najavits, L. 2002. *Seeking safety: A treatment manual for PTSD and substance abuse.* New York: Guilford Press.

Najavits, L., R. Weiss, S. Reif, D. Gastfriend, L. Siqueland, J. Barber, S. Butler, M. Thase, and J. Blaine. 1998. The addiction severity index as a screen for trauma and post-traumatic stress disorder. *Journal of the Study of Alcohol* 59 (1): 56–62.

Najavits, L., R. Weiss, and S. Shaw. 1997. The link between substance abuse and post-traumatic stress disorder in women: A research review. *American Journal on Addictions* 6 (4): 273–83.

National Center on Child Abuse and Neglect. 1998. *Child maltreatment 1996: Reports from the states for the national child abuse and neglect data system.* Washington, D.C.: U.S. Department of Justice.

National Coalition Against Domestic Violence. 2000. Denver, Colo. http://www.ncadv.org (accessed 2 July 2003).

Owen, B., and B. Bloom. 1995. Profiling women prisoners: Findings from national survey and California sample. *The Prison Journal* 75 (2): 165–85.

Pollock, J. 2002. *Women, prison and crime.* Pacific Grove, Calif.: Brooks/Cole.

Rapping, E. 1996. *The culture of recovery.* Boston: Beacon Press.

Ringel, C. 1997. *Criminal victimization in 1996, changes 1995–1996 with trends 1993–1996.* Washington, D.C.: U.S. Department of Justice, Bureau of Justice Statistics.

Roberts, A. R. 1998. *Battered women and their families: Intervention strategies and treatment programs.* 2d ed. New York: Springer Publishing.

Root, M. 1992. Within, between and beyond race. In *Racially mixed people in America,* edited by M. Root, 3–11. Thousand Oaks, Calif.: Sage Publications.

———. 1997. Women of color and traumatic stress in "domestic captivity": Gender and race as disempowering statues. In *Ethnocultural aspects of posttraumatic stress disorder issues, research and clinical applications,* edited by Anthony J. Marsella et al. Washington, D.C.: American Psychological Association.

Steele, C. 2000. Providing clinical treatment to substance abusing trauma survivors. *Alcohol Treatment Quarterly* 18 (3): 72.

Stern, D. 1985. *The interpersonal world of the infant.* New York: Basic Books.

Teicher, M. H. 2002. Scars that won't heal: The neurobiology of child abuse. *Scientific American,* March.

Teusch, R. 1997. Substance-abusing women and sexual abuse. In *Gender and addictions: Men and women in treatment,* edited by S. L. A. Straussner and E. Zelvin, 97–122. Northvale, N.J.: Jason Aronson, Inc.

Tower, C. 1993. *Understanding child abuse and neglect.* Boston: Allyn and Bacon.

Triffleman, E. 1998. Trauma, PTSD and substance abuse. In *Dual diagnosis and treatment.* 2d ed, edited by H. R. Kranzler and B. J. Rounsaville, 263–316. New York: Marcel Dekker.

United Nations General Assembly. 1993. *Declaration on the elimination of violence against women.* A/RES/48/104. New York: United Nations. http://www.un.org/documents/ga/res/48/a48r104.htm (accessed 5 November 2002).

U.S. Department of Justice. 2000. *Extent, nature, and consequences of intimate partner violence.* Washington, D.C.: Office of Justice Programs.

van der Kolk, B. 1996. The body keeps the score: Approaches to the psychobiology of posttraumatic stress disorder. In *Traumatic stress: The effects of overwhelming experience on mind, body, and society,* edited by B. A. van der Kolk, A. C. MacFarlane, and L. Weisaeth, 214–41. New York: Guilford Press.

Walters, M. 1990. The co-dependent Cinderella who loves too much . . . fights back. *The Family Therapy Networker,* July–August, 53–7.

Wells, T. 1970, 1972. Woman—Which includes man, of course: An experience in awareness. In *Issues in Feminism,* edited by S. Ruth. Columbus, Ohio: McGraw-Hill.

Whitfield, C. 1995 *Memory and abuse: Remembering and healing from trauma.* Pompano Beach, Fla.: Health Communications, Inc.

Winfield, I., L. George, M. Swartz, and D. Blazer. 1990. Sexual assault and psychiatric disorders among a community sample of women. *American Journal of Psychiatry* 147 (3): 335–41.

Winnecott, D. W. 1965. *The maturational process and the facilitation environment: Studies in the theory of emotional development.* New York: International University Press, Inc.

FEEDBACK FORM

Dear Group Facilitator:

I would appreciate hearing about your experience with the *Beyond Trauma* program. Any information you would like to share with me will be greatly appreciated.

Describe yourself.

_____

_____

_____

Describe where you facilitated this program.

_____

_____

_____

Describe your experience with the *Beyond Trauma* program.

_____

_____

_____

What did you find most useful?

_____

_____

_____

What did you find least useful?

_____

_____

_____

Why? How?

_____

_____

_____

Other suggestions/comments:

_____

_____

_____

Thank you for your input.

Please return this form to:

Stephanie S. Covington, Ph.D., LCSW
Center for Gender & Justice
Institute for Relational Development
7946 Ivanhoe Avenue, Suite 201B
La Jolla, CA 92037

FAX: (858) 454-8598
E-mail: SSCIRD@aol.com

ABOUT THE AUTHORS

Stephanie S. Covington, Ph.D., LCSW

Stephanie S. Covington is a clinician, lecturer, and organizational consultant. She has over twenty-four years of experience in the design and implementation of treatment services for women and is recognized for her pioneering work in both the public and private sectors. Her consulting work ranges from the development of women's treatment programs at the Betty Ford Center and at Hanley-Hazelden in West Palm Beach to the creation of gender-responsive treatment for the Pennsylvania Department of Corrections. Educated at Columbia University and the Union Institute, she has conducted seminars for health professionals, business and community organizations, and recovery groups in the United States, Mexico, Europe, Africa, and New Zealand. Dr. Covington is based in La Jolla, California, where she is co-director of both the Institute for Relational Development and the Center for Gender and Justice.

Marcia K. Morgan, Ph.D.

Marcia Morgan has worked with women's and girls' issues in criminal justice since 1975. Her passion is in research, training, curriculum development, and other special projects around women's and girls' issues. Marcia has written five curricula on women offenders for the National Institute of Corrections and the *Beyond Gender Barriers* curriculum for the Office of Juvenile Justice and Delinquency Prevention. She is a criminal justice consultant with Migima Designs in Portland, Oregon.

Other books by Stephanie S. Covington:

Leaving the Enchanted Forest:
The Path from Relationship Addiction to Intimacy

A Woman's Way through the 12-Steps

A Woman's Way through the 12-Steps Workbook

Awakening Your Sexuality: A Guide for Recovering Women

Helping Women Recover: A Program for Treating Addiction
(with a special edition for use in the criminal justice system)